T0208734

Experiences
of a Lifetime

Donald Brown

WESTBOW
P R E S S®
A DIVISION OF THOMAS NELSON
& ZONDERVAN

Copyright © 2019 Donald Brown.

All rights reserved. No part of this book may be used or reproduced by
any means, graphic, electronic, or mechanical, including photocopying,
recording, taping or by any information storage retrieval system
without the written permission of the author except in the case of
brief quotations embodied in critical articles and reviews.

Scripture quotations are taken from the Revised Standard Version of
the Bible, copyright © 1946, 1952, and 1971 the Division of Christian
Education of the National Council of the Churches of Christ in the
United States of America. Used by permission. All rights reserved.

WestBow Press books may be ordered through booksellers or by contacting:

WestBow Press
A Division of Thomas Nelson & Zondervan
1663 Liberty Drive
Bloomington, IN 47403
www.westbowpress.com
1 (866) 928-1240

Because of the dynamic nature of the Internet, any web addresses or
links contained in this book may have changed since publication and
may no longer be valid. The views expressed in this work are solely those
of the author and do not necessarily reflect the views of the publisher,
and the publisher hereby disclaims any responsibility for them.

Any people depicted in stock imagery provided by Getty Images are
models, and such images are being used for illustrative purposes only.
Certain stock imagery © Getty Images.

ISBN: 978-1-9736-5366-0 (sc)
ISBN: 978-1-9736-5367-7 (hc)
ISBN: 978-1-9736-5365-3 (e)

Library of Congress Control Number: 2019901728

Print information available on the last page.

WestBow Press rev. date: 3/26/2019

Contents

Dedication

I wish to dedicate this book to my wife, Nora, who died August 19, 2017 after 68 years as a faithful wife and a wonderful mother to our children, Gary and Jeannette.

Nora was an effective ministry and prayer partner. She loved the Lord; she loved music and she loved people.

Nora was a part of many of the experiences recorded in this book. Although I miss her, she is at home with the loving Father and His Son, Jesus Christ.

Introduction

At the age of 88 I have decided to write about various experiences I have had over the years. I have made a life application and appropriate scripture reference for each of these events in the hope that the reader will receive a practical benefit. They are not in a chronological or subject order because I think interest is added by reading a variety of experiences with differing life applications, even in short reading sessions. Some experiences are not dramatic, but they illustrate that life lessons can be learned even from simple situations. If you are a teacher, Bible study leader, public speaker or preacher you may find some of these accounts useful as illustrations. You may see personal benefit for your own life, or simply read them for enjoyment.

The Lord has been good to me over the years and has provided a variety of experiences from which I will attempt to extract some lessons for living a life that will honor our Lord.

All scripture references are quoted from the Revised Standard Version (RSV) of the Bible. In the quotations, the capital letters used in pronouns relating to God are my addition.

An Exciting Experience with the Ute Tribe

It was an exciting evening, filled with potential danger, education and excitement. It took place on the Ute Indian reservation near Cortez, Colorado in the fall of 1948. In fact Cortez is on the reservation but the encampment is back in the mountains nearby. About 1949 I looked up the Ute tribe in an Encyclopedia and it said this was one of the few remaining uncivilized tribes in the U.S. I don't know how old the encyclopedia was. A sacred mountain for the tribe is named the Sleeping Ute. From a distance it seems to have the outline of a man lying down. The superstition handed down is that one day the sleeping Ute will wake up and walk. Of course, I doubt that anyone really believed it would happen.

At the time, my dad, Solon Brown was pastor of Calvary Baptist Church in Cortez. He heard a rumor that the Utes would have a sun dance in thanks to the sun god for the harvest they had gathered. This would last for three days and three nights without their eating or drinking anything. This ceremony was only for the tribe, not the public. Dad and I decided to go on the second night. I was a senior in high school. A couple who lived up the street from us had just moved to Cortez from New York. They thought it sounded exciting and asked if they could go with us. We said they could. They didn't know what they were in for.

That evening we set out in our 1937 Pontiac to find the sun dance. We should have exercised some caution. A story circulated that from time to time a non-Indian would be found dead on the mountain (Sleeping Ute) considered holy to the tribe. We drove down arroyo beds where there were no roads. Soon we heard the chants of the ceremony. We went too far in one direction and the chants were behind us. In a clearing we were turning around and the engine died. The Pontiac had just been overhauled and the heated engine was tight. The starter would not turn it, so we got out the crank and tried. We could stand on the crank and still it would not move. The couple from New York was scared. About that time (around 9 or 10 P.M.) an Indian man on a horse rode into the edge of the clearing and just sat there for about a minute and rode off. The New York couple was more scared.

Dad and I decided to hike toward the chants and get help. The New York couple was "between a rock and a hard place." They were afraid to go and afraid to stay by themselves. They decided to stay in the car. Dad and I let the tom-tom beats guide us to the spot. We found the chief who had the only motorized vehicle there, a flatbed truck. He could speak enough English for us to communicate our problem. He rounded up 4 men and took us to the car. They gave us a push and the car started; back then the cars had metal bumpers that stood out from the body. We were on our way. We followed the truck to the site. We had forgotten to ask if it was ok to witness their dance.

When we got out of the car, the chief was standing there. Dad asked if it would be ok for us to observe their ceremony. The chief asked, "Umm how many?" I said, "There are four of us." He said, "Umm, dollar." I gave him a dollar and we had the freedom to observe as we wished. Many wagons and horses were in the camp.

In recent research I found how fortunate we were. An item on the website, *https://cafe-babylon.net*, states that Wendye Davis adopted a Ute baby that had been abused before birth and could not return to the tribe from the hospital. Some years later, as the child grew, an effort was made to help the child get familiar with her roots. They had become well acquainted with the tribal chief.

The chief, knowing that the child was a full blood Ute, convinced the other leaders to allow Wendye and daughter to attend the Sun Dance ceremony.

Some leaders from another Ute tribe arrived and objected to Wendye's presence at this sacred ceremony. They insisted on a meeting of all the tribal leaders present. The chief would not back down so the leaders from the other tribe left. This, the most sacred of all their ceremonies, was only for Utes.

Now, it seems that we may have been the only full non-Ute group to have attended such an event. However, further research has revealed that changes have now been made. In the late 1970s congress passed the American Indian Religious Freedom act, making the Sun Dance legal in the United States. It had been illegal. Today, non-Utes are permitted to witness the event, but with restrictions. At *www.southernute-nsn.gov/* I found that women in their menstrual cycle or pregnant cannot be on the Sun Dance grounds. Drugs and alcohol are not permitted. Cameras, tape or video recorders, food or water are not allowed near the area. No metal chairs are allowed, and no cell phones.

The website *www.thoughtco.com* gives some cautions: "You may see things at a Sun Dance which seem strange to you or even make you uncomfortable. Remember that this is a sacred event, and even if the practices are different from yours – and they probably will be – you should see it as a learning experience. Father William Stolzman, a Jesuit priest who spent many years living on Native American reservations, wrote in his book, <u>The Pipe and Christ</u>, 'Some people have great difficulty understanding and appreciating the tearing of flesh that takes place in the Sun Dance. Many cannot understand that there are higher values for which health is to be sacrificed.'"

Back to the event we attended. The tearing of flesh from lines attached to a man's chest by incision as he dances around the Sun Pole with increasing tension, or dancers cutting themselves, for example, did not happen the night we were there. They perhaps happened during the day. That night was calmer.

When we attended, there was a large enclosure made of posts. Inside the enclosure a group of adults sat near the Sun Pole waving branches over their heads to keep the evil spirits away. Six men were seated around a huge tom-tom, beating it and constantly chanting. The youth were around the edges of the enclosure and were responsible for keeping the fire going. In the center was the Sun Pole. It was a tree with the limbs cut off and painted up much like a barbershop pole. Others of all ages were with the wagons, waiting their turns for being a part of the action.

About every 10 minutes, the highly decorated sun dancer with a large mask over his head, blowing a type of flute that had colored streamers attached, would come out of an enclosure and dance to the Sun Pole. Then he would dance backward to the enclosure where he would stay until the next time. As I stated earlier, this went on for three days and three nights without stopping and without their eating and or drinking anything. I was chewing gum. A high school teenager with a sense of humor came over and said, "Did anyone tell you that you are not supposed to chew gum? Someone might see you and take it away from you." I swallowed the gum. We were able to move around some if we wished. The New York couple never moved. I'm not sure if they even breathed. It was the second night of the ceremony. We stayed until around one o'clock in the morning. The car engine had cooled and it started with no problem, so we returned home – a relief for the New York couple.

Here was a tribe of people who were willing to involve themselves in a sacrificial way to give thanks to the "one" they believed was responsible for their abundant crops. Those Native Americans needed Christ, but they knew there was a higher power that caused the seed to sprout and the crops to grow. They worshipped what they thought was that power. Today many in the tribes still worship that way, but through mission efforts many have come to know the truly powerful One and their superstitions are no longer needed.

How much energy do we go through to thank the true God, the One who put life in the seeds, nutrients in the soil, sends the sunshine and the rain, in addition to giving us eternal life with Him? Do you thank Him for the air you breathe, the food you eat and the loving care He gives? Are you thankful enough to share the Good News with others?

Nehemiah used two large choirs in giving thanks to the Lord (chapter 12). Timothy tells us that food is to be received with thanksgiving (I Tim. 4:3b). Psalm 100:4 says *"...give thanks to Him and praise His name."* And 1 Thessalonians 5:16-18 says, *"Be joyful always; pray continually; give thanks in all circumstances, for this is God's will for you in Christ Jesus."*

Farmington Revival

Although I had athletic scholarships offered in football, basketball and track, in three different colleges, I had previously decided that I would go to Oklahoma Baptist University. That's where I began my college career. I would hitch-hike back and forth between home in Cortez, Colorado and school in Shawnee, Oklahoma.

On one trip returning home I arrived at Farmington, New Mexico late in the evening so I decided to spend the night in the bus station and continue the next morning. First Baptist Church in Farmington was having a revival (evangelistic services). I decided to attend. After a dynamic message, the invitation (an appeal for anyone making a decision to come forward) was given. I turned to the man standing beside me and asked him, "Do you know Jesus as your Savior?" Without further discussion or comment, he immediately went forward. He made the decision to receive Jesus Christ as Lord of his life. After the service was over, several people came to me and said, "We have been praying for this man for years. God placed you here for this very purpose."

Has God urged you to witness to a particular person or minister to a special need and you just passed by that open door? That has happened to me. Doesn't that just gnaw at your soul? Perhaps now is the time to respond. God may re-open a door you missed – if it isn't too late. Then there are other doors He will open for you. Be sure to enter and address the need. Even the faithful disciples, Peter and John must have felt they had missed opportunities, for in Acts 4:29 they prayed, *"...enable your servants to speak your word with great boldness."* Do you need to pray for boldness in sharing God's good news?

Crooked Rows
Made Straight

When I was a young teenager, I worked on a ranch near Milnesand, New Mexico during the summers. Milnesand was a "wide spot in the road" between Portales and Hobbs. It had a Baptist Church and a store containing the post office. The surrounding area consisted of ranches and farms. While working on the ranch I also did some planting for a neighboring rancher. Those rows were extremely long. I remember my first day planting. As I approached the end of the row, the owner and another man were standing there, laughing and looking back behind me. I turned and looked. The rows were really crooked. I had been looking down in front of the tractor trying to follow the previous row, which was already crooked. From that experience I learned that if I would set my sight on a proper spot far ahead and move directly toward it, my rows straightened out.

As Christians, we are planting seeds of the Gospel as we move about in the world. If we try to do it all under our own power and direction, our rows will be crooked and the impact will not be good. If we keep our eyes upon Jesus Christ and let Him direct our paths, our rows in life will straighten out and the impact will be good.

Are you planting seeds of the gospel, or perhaps watering & cultivating, or reaping what God makes grow? Our mission includes each of these. The apostle Paul said, concerning his work at Corinth, "I planted the seed, Apollos watered it, but God made it grow" (1 Cor. 3:6). God puts the life in the seed and He is waiting for you to plant it or cultivate it.

Threatened in Egypt's Great Pyramid

In the 1980's Nora and I were with a group on a trip to the Holy Lands, including Israel, Jordan and Egypt. In Egypt we visited the Great Pyramid. Some of us rode a camel from the city of Cairo to the pyramid; others rode in the bus. We never dreamed we would experience anything like the event that took place.

Before relating our experience, let me share some information about this pyramid. The Great Pyramid in Egypt was built in 2575-2566 BC for Pharaoh Khufu (Greek: Cheops). "One hundred thousand people worked on the great structure for three months of each year, during the Nile's annual flood when it was impossible to farm the land and most of the population was unemployed. The pharaoh provided good food and clothing for his workers, and was kindly remembered in folk tales for many centuries," (Mark Millmore at *https://discoveringegypt.com/pyramids-temples-of-egypt/pyramids-of-giza/*).

The pyramid is a part of a group called the Giza Pyramids, located just outside of Cairo on the west bank of the Nile River. At one time these were included in the Seven Wonders of the World.

The Great Sphinx is also nearby. OK, that's enough of a history lesson – back to the experience.

After entering the pyramid we started up the ladder to the room at the top where the body of Khufu was entombed. About half way up, all the lights went out. The dark was so thick you could almost feel it. Many of those going up panicked and started feeling their way back down and out! I called out, "Are we going back to the bus?" I heard a voice I recognized saying "No," so I waited and before long the lights came on. As it turned out only six of us, other than the camel driver, continued to the top – three men and three women. As we were observing the tomb and surroundings, we became aware of three young men with clubs. They forced us over against the wall. We put the women behind us. Our camel driver took off & headed back down.

I figured our cameras, tape recorders, and perhaps our money would be taken and hoped that would be all. The men holding us stepped closer to the tomb, evidently to discuss their plans. We happened to be right in front of the ladder leading down. I said "Let's go." We started down and made it out. Other observers had started up and were in view to the three holding us so we were able to escape. This gang of three had caused the light outage, evidently hoping for a chance to get some valuables and money. Our bus driver said there has been an incident similar to this about once a year.

The rest of our group was waiting in the bus. The whole event took a long time. They were anxious and worried. The delay made us late for the tour of the museum at Memphis. The museum was closed, but our lady bus driver was a professor at Cairo University and had a lot of clout. She had called and arranged for us to have a private tour of everything, as long as we wished. We browsed both the outside museum and the inside museum. The inside consisted of a two story structure with a giant statue of Ramses II in the middle of the first floor.

The Lord was good to us. He led us out of a dangerous situation and provided a tour that was better than we would have experienced if everything had been on schedule. Sometimes we tend to question God when life events seem scary or unpleasant. But if we will simply trust Him, He may have something waiting that is better than we would ever expect. Also sometimes He may put us in uncomfortable situations to cause us to turn to Him and trust Him. As He leads us safely through, our faith is strengthened. In James 1:2-4 the writer says, *"Consider it pure joy, my brothers, whenever you face trials of many kinds, because you know that the testing of your faith develops perseverance. Perseverance must finish its work so that you may be mature and complete, not lacking anything."*

Isolation on the Ranch

As a teenager working on a ranch in New Mexico, one of my jobs was to ride the fences to check for barbwire breaks and to repair them. I treasured those times alone, sometimes a mile or more from the nearest house or any other person, just my horse and I. Those times were frequently used for praying aloud. I could be as loud as I wanted to be in pouring out my heart to God. No one but God would hear me. Sometimes that isolation is hard to come by in our world today. But we need to make an effort to provide some kind of private time.

There is power in prayer. If your heart is right, God will listen & He will answer in a way that is to your ultimate benefit & fits His plan for your life. It may not be the answer you hoped for, but He knows the future & He knows you better than you know yourself.

Often we are so busy we forget to pray & when we do, it is on the run. But God tells us in Psalm 46:10, *"Be still and know that I am God."* If we will do that, we can experience, as the song reminds us, a sweet hour of prayer. In Ephesians 4:6 Paul says, *"Do not be anxious about anything, but in everything, by prayer and petition, with thanksgiving, present your requests to God."* Do you need to make some changes in your prayer life?

Opportunity in a Church Fire

Leaving a pastorate in Dallas, we (Nora and I and our children, Gary and Jeannette) went to Maryland where I assumed the pastorate of a church at Kingsville, north of Baltimore. The Lord had instilled in me the missionary spirit my dad had possessed. A few years later, some birds got into the old electrical wiring, near a junction box, of the church building and built a nest. One night a fire resulted and, in addition to the fire trucks, a crowd gathered. Bobby, one of our high school youth, saw a great opportunity. He ran into the burning building, grabbed some gospel tracts and handed them out in the crowd. The judgment about entering a burning building may not have been so good, but his motive was right – and he acted on what he felt God directing him to do.

No matter what our age or circumstances in life may be, God gives us opportunities that we often pass by. Does this happen to you? It has happened to me – too often. In Acts 4:29 Peter and John asked the Lord to give them courage to speak God's word boldly. Maybe we need to pray for courage, so we will make the best of those opportunities for God's glory. In acts 1:8 Jesus instructs us to be His witnesses. In Matthew 28:19 Christ said, *"...go and make disciples... ,"* and Paul tells us that our hope in Jesus Christ will give us boldness. After speaking of the glory of our ministry that brings righteousness, he said, *"Therefore, since we have such a hope, we are very bold."* So let's ask for boldness and wisdom as God shows us the opportunities He has provided. Bobby did just that. What about you?

The Switchblade Knife

When I was pastor of First Baptist Church, Kingsville Maryland, one day Roy, a high school teenager, came to my office and asked the question that is rarely asked alone. He said, "How can I be saved?" I shared with him the way of salvation. Then Roy stood up, reached in his pocket and pulled out his switchblade knife. He pressed the button and the blade flew open. He then closed the knife and handed it to me. He said, "I won't need this anymore. I'm trusting Jesus." Previously, if a situation got out of hand Roy had his switchblade to rely on. No more! Now he had the Lord Jesus to trust.

Roy was a friend of our son, Gary. They were both seniors in high school. Gary had been witnessing to Roy, and the Lord honored his effort by Roy's trip to my office and accepting Christ as the Lord of his life. He became active in our youth group. A little later he made a ceramic piece of the praying hands, like ones found in Christian book stores, brought it to our house and gave it to us as a gesture of his appreciation.

There's more to the story. Shortly after graduation Roy went into the military service. Soon, he came home on leave. He was in his Volkswagen, driving through those Maryland hills and turns, on his way to see his fiancé. He pulled out from behind a truck, evidently to see if it was safe to pass. He met an eighteen wheeler head on. I preached Roy's funeral. It was a military funeral.

Roy is in heaven now. If he had not made the switch from the knife to Christ, it is difficult to think where he would be. If Gary had not witnessed to him, perhaps he would never have made that all-important decision

Do you have a friend, or perhaps a family member or relative, or other opportunity God provides you of someone who needs you to show him/her the way to heaven? Ask God for courage to share. In Ezekiel 3:18-19 God says, *"When I say to a wicked man, 'You will surly die, and you do not warn him or speak out to dissuade him from his evil ways in order to save his life, that wicked man will die for his sin, and I will hold you accountable for his blood. But if you warn the wicked man and he does not turn from his evil ways, he will die for his sin; but you will have saved yourself."*

Our responsibility is to share. The responsibility for decision falls on the person with whom we are sharing. Do you know someone who needs your personal witness so that life will gain purpose and meaning in this world and he or she will go to be with the Lord forever when time on this earth is over?

A Secret Gift

When I was a pastor in Dallas, I visited a family that I knew was having a rough time. —sickness, loss of income and school was starting. But there was no money to buy the children's needed shoes & clothes. They told me about one of my deacons who had visited them. He and his wife provided new shoes and some clothes for all of the children and had brought a large bag of groceries to the family. Evidently, the deacon & his wife told no one about this, and I had not known about it. However, I did let the deacon & his wife know that the family expressed great appreciation and that I was proud of them.

Over forty years later during my retirement from Southern Baptist home missions (now called North American missions) and as director of two associations in Maryland we were back in Texas, living in Sulphur Springs. One day I was shopping at Walmart. I was in the checkout line. When I started to pay for the groceries, the gentleman behind me said, "Don't take his money. I'm paying." I had not noticed who was behind me. It was the high school band director. I don't think he ever told anyone, but I did. I shared it with the Sunday school department I directed.

The band director's action inspired me. A short time later I was at Arby's, which is located in a truck stop. The truck stop is also a Greyhound bus station. The man in front of me had come off the bus headed for Dallas. He seemed to be a person who might be hard-pressed for funds. After he ordered his meal and handed the cashier his money I said, "Give him his money back. I'm paying."

The band director's action really got me searching about my own use of the money the Lord has entrusted to me. I've talked to the Lord about it. I have passed up so many opportunities to help. Sometimes I have bought food or gas when I would not give money, not knowing how money would be used. But I have failed to accept many opportunities for ministry that God has placed before me.

On another day, sometime later, after I had finished my workout at the ROC (Recreation and Outreach Center) of First Baptist church, a young man with a backpack was sitting in a chair next to where I was going to sit with a cup of coffee to cool off. We began to talk. He never asked for money or any favors, but I sensed by his clothing and general demeanor that he was going through difficult times. I asked about his job. He said he was unemployed. I asked where he lived. He said right now he did not have a place. Because of my wife's hospice care I could not invite him home, but gave him a location where I felt he could get help. Others were coming in after their workouts and sitting around.

The Lord really gripped me this time. I had made so many excuses in the past. I inconspicuously slipped a $20 bill from my wallet, rolled it up and, as our chairs were side by side, held my hand down between them, and whispered, "Just between us." He glanced at what was in my hand and his expression showed an obvious thanks.

The deacon and the band director did not share about their gifts. I finally shared about the gift at Arby's in a Sunday School Class of about 8 or 9. It was a discussion in which I thought it could help, but I also shared that I was inspired by the band director's action. I am now sharing with you about the young man at the ROC because I feel it might encourage you.

Deuteronomy 10:14, Psalm 24:1 and 1 Corinthians 10:26 all tell us that the earth and everything in it belongs to the Lord. The Psalm verse specifically includes us. And 2 Corinthians 1:21-22 says, *"… He anointed us, set His seal of ownership on us, and put His Spirit in our hearts as a deposit, guaranteeing what is to come."*

The money He trusts us with is not ours. It is the Lord's. We are His stewards. Does this speak to your situation? How are you using the Lord's money & other possessions He has put in your care? Is there someone with a special need who needs your caring assistance?

Stadium Preaching As
a High Schooler

As a high schooler I was privileged to experience four years of varsity football and basketball. In those days there was no TV, network radio or much national coverage of sports in the newspapers. Area newspapers gave a lot of attention to sports.

A football scholarship was offered me at Ft. Lewis College in Durango, about 40 miles from Cortez, where I spent my senior year of high school. A basketball scholarship was offered at Adams State University, in Alamosa, while we were playing in the state tournament held there. But I already had decided I would go to Oklahoma Baptist University. Coach Hurt, at OBU, offered me a track scholarship, but I already had a ministerial scholarship there (both as a Baptist minister's son and as a licensed minister). I also needed to work and earn an income to provide for other living expenses.

Back to Cortez. Being the fullback on our team and also in the ministry are likely what led to my invitation in 1949 to preach a citywide early Easter service in the football stadium. I think all the churches participated.

Sometimes when we mention special blessings the Lord has given us, it sounds like bragging. But had there been the networking that exists today, perhaps none of my athletic awards would have happened. God knows the whole picture and if we are faithful in the opportunities He gives us, He will provide the opportunities for greater service. This is true no matter what your age may be. Jesus said, *"Ask and it will be given to you; seek and you will find; knock and the door will be opened to you"* (Matt. 7:7). What about the open doors God has put before you? Do you enter or walk on by?

A Shocking Experience

I still remember it! When I was in the first grade of Elementary School (about 1937) we lived in Melrose, New Mexico. My parents had a laundry in an old hotel building. The laundry was in the whole downstairs and we lived upstairs.

I remember one Sunday afternoon. I took my toy pistol and was running through the laundry poking it at, and in, whatever was convenient, "shooting" as I went. Light sockets were hanging from the ceiling throughout the laundry. Most had bulbs in them, but one was empty. As I was running by, I climbed upon a table and stuck my pistol up in the socket and started to say, "Bang!" But I received the bang. Sparks flew everywhere it seemed and I got a jolt I would not forget.

An important lesson comes to mind in this. Just as I was not expecting the shock I received and was having so much fun I had not given a thought about the danger lurking in the socket, Satan sneaks up on us when we are least aware and strikes us at our weakest point.

We must always be on guard and exercise the strength to not let Satan get a foothold. We cannot do it on our own. In Ephesians 3:16, the apostle Paul reminds us of the source of our strength. He said, *"I pray that out of His glorious riches He may strengthen you with power through His Spirit in your inner being".* Are you staying alert and relying on God's power to give you the strength to resist Satan's approaches?

Parental Lesson on Tithing

My parents set good examples for their children. For a couple of years or so, when I was a child, they owned a laundry in Melrose, New Mexico. Back then washing machines were the ringer type. After the clothes were washed by agitating in the machine, they were fed through a ringer to the first rinse tub. Then the ringer would be swung around to the second rinse tub and the clothes were fed through it to that one, which often had some bluing added to the water. After running the clothes through the ringer from the second tub, they were hung out on the line to dry, or generally the customer would take the clothes and hang them on their own clothes line at home. There were no automatic washers or driers.

I was paid a penny for each machine I emptied and cleaned. Back in the 1930s a penny was worth many times what it is today. In fact New Mexico had a tax coin called a mill. It was worth a tenth of a penny. The great depression had its toll on the lives of people.

My parents were dedicated tithers. Mom used to say, "I had rather have nine tenths with God's blessing that ten tenths without it." They also were faithful in contributing to mission efforts, and when a missionary would speak at our church, he or she would stay in our home, eating and sleeping there.

Mom told me that every other penny should go to the church. I was too young to think of the difference between 10 and 50 percent. She knew what she was doing – instilling in me at an early age my responsibility to God, even with my possessions. Sometimes a customer would toss some pennies on the floor for me and say I could have them, or would hand me a penny or two. One doctor would toss some coins on the floor and often include a nickel or two. I remember someone gave me a penny and I said, "This one goes to the church." I must have had a look or tone in my voice that implied, "Do you have another one." He gave me another one.

With the tithing principle instilled in me by my parents, when I got older I was faithful in this. Throughout our married life Nora and I have always returned to God, through His church, at least a tenth of our income in addition to the various mission offerings and other special offerings and needs. In fact, for the last forty or so years we have given a minimum of 11 or more instead of 10 percent, not to be legalistic, but if we do not set standards we are likely to trickle down in our giving. Our children have followed our example.

It is important that parents instill Christian principles in their children at early ages – and be sure they recognize those principles in their parents. The Lord tells us in Deut. 11:18-19, *"Fix these words of mine in your hearts and minds; … Teach them to your children, talking about them when you sit at home and when you walk along the road, when you lie down and when you get up"*.

Diversion from Ministry

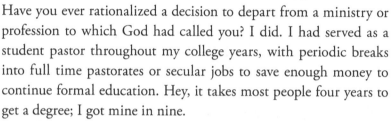

Have you ever rationalized a decision to depart from a ministry or profession to which God had called you? I did. I had served as a student pastor throughout my college years, with periodic breaks into full time pastorates or secular jobs to save enough money to continue formal education. Hey, it takes most people four years to get a degree; I got mine in nine.

After Nora and I had completed our college degrees in New Mexico, we moved to Fort Worth, Texas with my intention to enter the seminary. Nora secured a teaching position and I got a job selling debit insurance. I planned on entering the seminary, but was promoted to assistant manager. I thought I would only delay entry for a semester or two, but was soon promoted as manager of the company's office in a developing area of Fort Worth. The added income would make it easier for the time I would be in the seminary with only Nora's income to support us, so I accepted the promotion.

After a year in the insurance business, which I really did not enjoy, I found employment as a pharmaceutical detailer, calling on doctors. That was an enjoyable experience, but I still planned on getting my seminary education. Bentex pharmaceutical was a rapidly growing company and in about three months I was promoted to district manager for Texas and Oklahoma. This would be only a temporary delay I thought, so I accepted the position. Now for the biggie.

After about four months as district manager, I was asked to be the national sales director. This would involve moving to the home office in Houston. I was faced with a major decision. I rationalized that God can use men in business. He can, but is that where He wanted me? I do not remember praying about the matter.

I accepted the promotion and a few months later the board of directors elected me as vice president, in addition to the national sales director position. I thought I had a good thing going. God had other plans!

After a couple of years, I developed pericarditis and was in intensive care for two weeks. At one point I spoke to our children, telling them to be sure and obey their mom, for it seemed my time on earth was ending. You have probably heard the expression, "You have to hit a mule over the head with a two-by-four to get its attention." Now the Lord had me where I would listen. My physician at Methodist Hospital was the internationally known Dr. Denton Cooley who, in South Africa, did the first successful heart transplant. The Almighty watches over His own! After a few years, even scar tissue could not be detected on an EKG.

The Lord convinced me that His plan for me in a career ministry is permanent. When I started telling Nora about the decision God had led me to make, she was planning to tell me that God had convinced her of the same thing.

This was in March. The company president visited me when I was in a private room at the hospital. I shared with him our decision. He extended my insurance for three months and told me to hang on to the company car until I was able to look for one to replace it.

We moved to Fort Worth where Nora obtained a teaching position and I enrolled in an evangelism course, taught by Dr. Roy Fish, at the Southwestern Baptist Theological Seminary. While working on the Master of Divinity (MDiv) degree I became pastor of Fireside Drive Baptist Church in Dallas.

After completing the degree, we moved to Union Bridge, Maryland upon being called as pastor of First Baptist Church there. God had impressed upon me that He wanted me in a pioneer area for evangelistic churches. The church in Maryland permitted me to be gone for a month at a time while completing my doctor of ministry (DMin.) degree at Midwestern Baptist Theological Seminary in Kansas City, Missouri, using their mini-semesters.

At each mini-semester we would focus on one subject area for a month instead of changing classes every hour. In preparation for each semester, we would be required to read and report on six to eight books assigned by the seminary. Often well known writers in the subject area would be enlisted to lecture in many of the morning or afternoon classes.

After six years at Union Bridge, I was called to be director of missions for two Southern Baptist Associations. This was a cooperative position among the associations' churches, the Baptist Convention of Maryland/Delaware and the Home Mission Board (now North American Mission Board). Nora and I were appointed missionaries and we were in Maryland a total of 27 years (six as pastor, 20 as DOM/missionaries and one year after retirement). Nora taught school for six years in Maryland, then retired and served 20 years as my administrative assistant. Camp David, the president's retreat, was in one of my associations.

About ten or twelve years after leaving Bentex, I attended the annual Southern Baptist Convention, as had been my practice for several years. This time it was held in Houston. The former president of Bentex, "Coke" Reeves and his wife, invited me to dinner in their home. The company had expanded so rapidly it got the attention of some of the larger umbrella type companies. One of them had purchased Bentex. Coke told me, "If you had remained with Bentex, you would be quite wealthy now, as the executives of the company were treated handsomely." I was glad he said that, for I had no regret. There was not even an inkling of feeling that I would like to have received that. I think God wanted me to hear it to further confirm that I was where He wanted me to be.

We retired from the two associations at the end of 1995, not from ministry, just from employment. We moved to Sulphur Springs Texas at the end of 1996 to be close to our kids and grandkids. The

Lord has kept us busy, both in First Baptist Church and preaching assignments elsewhere. You never retire from the ministry, just from an employed position. Twenty-two years later I am 88 years old and Nora's age was 85when she went to be with the Lord last year. She used her gifts faithfully in ministry and was a great companion to me.

Even when we wander away, God may use events and situations we face to prepare us for the next step in His plan. He sees the whole picture. I grew up being shy around people with high educational degrees or high positions in government or companies. As I called on doctors and associated with company presidents and others with high positions, God broke all those barriers down and prepared me for the future. I found that no matter the position they hold, it is simply a job that I consider to be on the level of other workers.

The message I wish to convey in all of this is first, the importance of following God's plan for your life. He has a plan for every life.

Second, if you have strayed from His plan it's not too late, no matter your age or position, to return. God knows your physical strength and abilities and He still has a plan for you. He will equip you for the task to which He calls you.

Paul says in Romans 12:11, *"Never be lacking in zeal, but keep your spiritual fervor, serving the Lord."* Sometimes, because of age or physical disability, your workload or method of service may change. God understands that. Remain true to your calling as God planed it at this stage of your life.

Hitchhiking to Camp

In 1949 western Colorado and New Mexico Southern Baptists were all a part of the New Mexico Baptist Convention as Colorado did not yet have a state convention. Enloe Youth Camp was the youth camp for all those churches. During the summer the various weeks at camp were assigned to different age groups.

Having completed my senior year of high school in Cortez, Colorado I decided to hitchhike to and from camp as I was the only one going from our church. Previously, when I lived in New Mexico, I had always been with a group and transportation was provided. I had a duffle bag with my bedding and clothes in it, and I set out. In those days people were not afraid to pick up hitchhikers. I know my dad did this often.

A semi-truck driver picked me up and carried me to Bloomfield, New Mexico, west of Farmington. He said that because of the long stretches of highway, he wanted someone to keep him awake.

At Bloomfield a family (man, his wife and high school age daughter) gave me a ride all the way to Estancia, south of Moriarty. On the way, the driver stopped for gas. Before he realized what was happening, I had paid for the fuel. This was a surprise and he said he had never heard of a hitchhiker paying for the gas. It was probably thought that I had no, or very little, money. But I worked at a hardware store during the summer and part-time the rest of the year. I think this family had planned to continue west at Moriarty but side-tracked to get me to Estancia where the road up the mountain to Enloe camp began. I think my paying for the gas may have influenced him to take me on to Estancia. Many vehicles were headed up the rather steep road to camp and as I started walking with my duffle bag one of them picked me up and took me the rest of the way.

The Lord teaches us to care for others. As we reach out in a caring way to others, not only are others blessed, God also extends special blessings to us. Paul, in Philippians 2:4-5, instructs us to give a helping hand to others. He says, *"Each of you should look not only to your own interests, but also to the interest of others. Your attitude should be the same as that of Christ Jesus."* Sometimes a kind act will lead the person you helped to be open to your sharing the Good News of Christ with him or her. The people in the car that gave me a ride were already solid Christians. In fact, their giving me a lift was doing what Paul, in the verses above, was talking about. Do any opportunities come to mind?

Four Corners, Four States

It's amazing! With all our fifty states, there is only one spot where four states come together. This is where Arizona, Utah, New Mexico and Colorado all connect. A monument is there. It is low enough that a person can bend over it and be in four states at the same time. My wife Nora, our children Gary and Jeannette and I did that. We each had one hand in Colorado and one in Utah while one foot was in New Mexico and the other one in Arizona. But what did this accomplish? Nothing but a memory. However, memories can lead to interesting conversations later.

Just like being in four states at one time, sometimes we find ourselves involved in so many things that we are not very effective in any. We don't have enough time or our minds are too divided. It is important that we set priorities and focus on those that are most important. This requires communication with God to seek His direction. The Psalmist found this to be true.

The writer of the 119th Psalm said in verse 133, *"Direct my footsteps according to your word."* As choices pile up on us, all seemingly good, we need God's direction for His assurance that we make the right choice. The Father has a plan for your life. Are you following His plan?

An Unusual Woman

While a student at Eastern New Mexico University I was pastor of Crossroads Baptist Church at Crossroads, New Mexico. This ranching and farming area had only one church and a store that also served as the post office. One of the ranches was owned by a widow who was about 80 years old. I remember once when Nora and I went to her house, she needed to feed the cattle. I accompanied her on this, thinking I could help. But she really didn't need help. Loose hay and a pitchfork were in the back of the pickup. As she drove through the pastures, when she came to an area for dispensing some hay, she would put the pickup in second gear and, while the vehicle is still moving, would crawl out of the cab and into the bed to toss out some hay. She would then crawl back into the cab and continue to the next area and repeat the action.

This lady was a dynamic Christian and member of the church. She aided the small church in so many ways, without drawing attention to herself. We established one Sunday night a month on which a Christian film would be shown. In the warm months this was at the community center, merely an open shelter with seats. This elderly widow, without telling anyone, provided money for purchasing a projector.

When we paved the parking lot, purchased pews and installed a baptistery, our lady waited until time for others to contribute, then quietly provided the rest of the money so that the church would not have a debt to pay off.

She evidently realized that, as Nora and I were both students, we didn't have much money. Often after service on Sunday night, as people were leaving and we were shaking hands, she would leave a hundred dollar bill in my hand. After graduation, Nora and I moved to Fort Worth. When our next wedding anniversary came, she sent a card with a hundred dollar bill in it.

This lady never talked about her gifts; she never bragged about her various good deeds. This is the type of person that is remembered. She was laying up treasures in heaven!

Jesus said, *"Do not store up for yourselves treasures on earth, where moth and rust destroy, and where thieves break in and steal. But store up for yourselves treasures in heaven, where moth and rust do not destroy, and where thieves do not break in and steal"* (Matt. 6:19-20.) Which account are you focused on?

From Gasoline to Wind

When my dad was pastor of the Baptist Church at Milnesand, New Mexico, the state did not have rural electrification. Like Crossroads, Milnesand was a ranching and farming area with one church and a store that also served as the post office.

For light on Sunday nights, when Dad first went there, we had gasoline lanterns hanging from the ceiling. A battery house with a bank of batteries inside and a wind charger on its roof were near the church building but had not been used for a few years. I don't know the reason.

Dad and a few men got everything in shape, including repairs to the wind charger. Light sockets already were suspended from the ceiling. All had pull chains and 12 volt bulbs. That's the voltage produced from the batteries, powered by the wind charger. With the winds on the plains of Eastern New Mexico, the batteries were kept charged during the week and we never were short on electricity and good lighting on Sunday nights.

Sometimes God has more for us than we're experiencing. But we may be unwilling to go and pick it up. We just follow the course of least resistance and hang up our gasoline lanterns. Wake up! Listen to God's Holy Spirit prodding you to get up and receive His blessings. Find out what God wants you to do and to be. That's where the blessings are stored.

The apostle Peter instructs, in 1 Peter, *"Like newborn babies, crave pure spiritual milk, so that by it you may grow up in your salvation ..."* Having any growing pains? Your spiritual muscles must be growing!

Playing Tag on Horses

When I was 14-15 years old, my dad was pastor of the Baptist church in a ranching and farming area of New Mexico. On Sunday afternoons we guys often played tag, among other things, on horses. The one who was "it" would have to tag someone riding another horse so that person would become "it." The maneuvering we sometimes were able to make to avoid contact was amazing. This reminds me of maneuvers some make today to avoid being "it."

Have you been tagged for a given responsibility, perhaps to an office in your Bible study class, or as a teacher of the class, or maybe a visitation chairperson in your church? The Lord has led someone or a group to select you. Do you maneuver around to avoid the tag? "Joe or Susie is better qualified; tag him or her." Or, "Sometimes we go out of town on Sundays and we would have to make changes in our plans. Someone else would be more dependable"

I'm not asking you to neglect family or overload to the point of being ineffective, but sometimes it may mean giving up one job for another – as when a Bible study teacher is asked to direct a department.

This happened to me. Being retired, I served as pastor supply for various churches in the association and beyond. I was also teaching a Bible study class in the church where I am a member. I would often need to get a substitute teacher. Later I was asked to direct a department. The Lord had solved my absence problem. After the opening assembly I still have time to get to any church in the association before the 11:00 worship. I only need to get a substitute when preaching farther away or for an earlier worship time. These occasional absences also provide an opportunity to train someone else for a leadership role. So, if God tags you for a job, He will equip you. Accept the new adventure!

We are told in Hebrews 13:31, *"May the God of peace, who through the blood of the eternal covenant brought back from the dead our Lord Jesus, that great Shepherd of the sheep, equip you with everything good for doing His will..."* Just trust Him. He will do it!

Uncover that Lord's Supper!

Back in the 1930s and 1940's, and before, the Lord's Supper trays were always covered with a table cloth until time to serve it. There was a reason. I'll share the reason after this little story. It is a popular one and no one seems to know who first told it or wrote it.

It is said that a young woman was hosting a dinner party for her friends and served a delicious pot roast. Someone at the party asked for the recipe and the young woman wrote it out and gave it to her.

After the friend looked over the recipe, she asked, "Why do you cut both ends off the roast before it is prepared and put in the pan?" The young woman replied, "I don't know. I learned this recipe from my mom and that's the way she always did it."

The next day the young woman called her mom to ask her, "Mom, when we make the pot roast, why do we cut off and dispose of the ends before putting it in the pan and seasoning it?" Her mom replied, "That is how your grandma always did it and I learned the recipe from her."

Then the young lady called her elderly grandma and asked her the same question: "Grandma, I often make the pot roast recipe that I learned from mom. She says she learned it from you. Why do you cut the ends off the roast before preparing it?" The grandmother replied, "I don't know why you do it; I cut them off because the roast was always bigger than the pan I had back then. I had to cut the ends off to make it fit."

Now, why do many churches still cover the Lord's Supper trays today? Who knows? But here is why we used to do it. Few churches had air conditioning. If they did, it would be a water cooled system installed in a window. Churches would normally have the windows and doors open, in warm or hot weather, and flies were a problem. The Lord's Supper would attract more flies. So, in addition to tray covers if available, a white table cloth covered the display.

Today, most churches have air conditioning, but we are victims of habit and don't know why we do some things. Some churches still cover the elements with a table cloth. I think it is because "That's the way we always did it." Let the people see the elements displayed! This can complement the sermon as the congregation meditates on Christ's great sacrifice for us. Tray lids are ok. Worshipers can still see the trays and meditate on what is in them.

Pounding the Evangelist

As a student in college, I was pastor of a church between Portales and Hobbs, New Mexico. One year for a revival meeting we invited the associational missionary (now called director of missions). Back then revival meetings usually continued for two weeks and could be extended if decisions were still being made.

The association only permitted our evangelist to receive revival pay from two churches each year. We were a small church and knew he would receive a much greater stipend from other churches, but he was willing to come without pay. Occasionally churches would give their pastor a "love pounding" or do the same for a guest speaker as part of the pay. The following took place at Crossroads Baptist Church.

At the conclusion of the series of meetings, on the final Sunday night, the members filled the evangelist's car with food items. These were canned goods, baked items, dairy products, and more. Most were items that could be stored for a long time without spoiling. It's good that he was alone that night because I don't think I have ever seen a car so packed with food. We knew the associational rule only applied to monetary pay and did not rule out a church showing appreciation in other ways.

Sometimes people volunteer to do demanding jobs for no pay. It is always good to show appreciation in a way that will benefit them and let them know you care and appreciate their effort. When you do this you will receive the greater blessing.

Paul says in Galatians 6:6, *"Anyone who receives instruction in the word must share all good things with his instructor."*

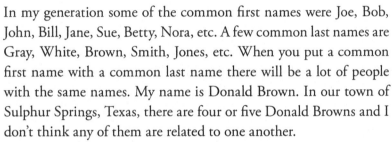

Common Name Problem

In my generation some of the common first names were Joe, Bob, John, Bill, Jane, Sue, Betty, Nora, etc. A few common last names are Gray, White, Brown, Smith, Jones, etc. When you put a common first name with a common last name there will be a lot of people with the same names. My name is Donald Brown. In our town of Sulphur Springs, Texas, there are four or five Donald Browns and I don't think any of them are related to one another.

In fact, in First Baptist Church there are two Donald Browns. Both of us are about the same age. People were often confused as to which Donald Brown is spoken of until they ask for the wife's name. One day, about 15 years ago, we both appeared at a restaurant at the same time and we talked about the confusion people have because of our same names. So we decided that I would be called Don and he would be called Donald. This has helped.

Back in my college days, I attended my first semester at Oklahoma Baptist University and one day I got a grocery bill that was three months past due. I had never charged anything at any grocery store. After some phone calls, the store personnel discovered they had mailed to the wrong Donald Brown. I don't know where they got my address.

When I was a student at Eastern New Mexico University, I started to take a final exam. The professor came to me and said, "You have an unpaid bill at the bookstore and I cannot give you the exam until it is paid." I replied that I had never charged anything at the bookstore, and after his making a call or two he discovered it was another Donald Brown.

That summer Nora (my wife) had decided to take some courses at the State Teachers' College in Las Vegas, New Mexico. I decided that, instead of twiddling my thumbs, I would enroll in a class. When I enrolled, a request for my transcript was sent. I was contacted and told that, because of my failing grades, I did not qualify for that course. I remembered the final exam and the unpaid bookstore bill and decided the school must have sent his transcript. Yep. The middle initial was different. The school sent the proper transcript and all was ok.

Do you have that problem? It may not be for a common name, but have you been the victim of false rumor? Or, does someone tag you with the lifestyle of a close friend, just because you are seen with that person? Christians are often with unbelievers whose lifestyles are considerately different. How else are we to win them to the Lord? There is a difference between regularly hanging out with groups whose ways are contrary to those of believers, and selecting a friend and showing that friend Christ's love. With a group, you need to have other solid believers with you.

How do you face such wrongful opinions or actions against you? Instead of responding in anger, in a kind way try to get at the root of the problem. Be sure your actions support the truth you are trying to communicate. Ephesians 4:26 tells us, *"In your anger do not sin."* Paul continues in verse 32, *"Be kind and compassionate to one another, forgiving each other, just as in Christ God forgave you."* OK, calm down.

Professor with an Eidetic Memory

After graduating from high school in 1949 I enrolled for the fall semester at Oklahoma Baptist University. At the faculty reception on the first evening, we were introduced to the faculty members. The faculty was in a line and the freshmen, perhaps between 100 & 200, were lined up to go through the line. A person would be introduced with just the first and last names to the first faculty member and that member would introduce to the next one. When I was going through the line one member said to Dr. Orin Cornet, "Dr. Cornet, this is Donald Brown." Dr. Cornet responded "Donald J. Brown from Cortez Colorado?"

Dr. Cornet had glanced trough all the enrollment cards and had them memorized. I heard him speak one time on eidetic memory and how he remembered things. He said, "When I meet someone I don't know and wish to remember the name, I picture a sign across the person with the name spelled out. If it's a name that has variant spellings, I ask how he or she spells the name. If I see the person two years later, I see the sign with the correct spelling. He said, "You can also remember some names by association." I tried this one a couple of years ago when I met a pastor whose last name was "Parrot." I pictured in my mind a parrot sitting on top of his head. When I would see him, my mind would picture the parrot on his head.

Is there a good way to remember scripture passages? I wish I knew. When I was young, my mind was sharper and I could fairly easily memorize long passages and their references. Now I tend to forget some of those I used to know. Also, some of them I can quote but do not remember the references.

We do need to memorize passages and their references for various situations – sharing the good news with others, helping us understand God's instructions for us at various times and assisting others in times of special need.

In his second letter to Timothy Paul complimented him on his knowledge of the Scripture. Then in 2 Timothy 3:16 Paul said, *"All Scripture is God-breathed and is useful for teaching, rebuking, correcting and training in righteousness, so that the man of God may be thoroughly equipped for every good work."*

Paul tells the members of the church at Colossae to, *"Let the word of Christ dwell in you richly as you teach and admonish one another with all wisdom …"* (Col. 3:16). 'Nuf said! Get the dust off that Bible and read it every day, and memorize some key verses. You will be more sensitive to God's Holy Spirit as He seeks to guide you each day.

Life as a Farm Kid

In the late 1930s and very early 1940s we lived on a farm just west of Portales, New Mexico, just across the lane from the H-Bar Ranch. I think the site later became the Portales Municipal Airport and a portion of the H-Bar Ranch became a country club.

Located in Portales were a tomato cannery, The McCasland Peanut Roastery (the largest in the nation, later bought by Sunland), a broom manufacturer, potato processing houses and a cotton gin. Most farms in the area were truck farms; that is, they raised crops to be trucked to the various processing plants.

On our farm we raised tomatoes (11 acres), cotton, potatoes, watermelons and popcorn, as well as providing a pasture for the livestock. The entire family worked the farm. When I was about 10 years old I would ride the knife sled to control weeds in the cotton patches. The knife sled had two runners that would run in the furrows and a seat on top. A knife extended from the outside of each runner and would slice just below the tops of the ridges on each side to kill the weeds. Later, a turning plow would fill in the furrows and the ridges became the furrows for the irrigation water to flow.

The knife sled was pulled by a team of two horses. I was too short to reach up to bridle and harness the horses. I would throw the reins around the horse's neck and pull the head down to bridle it. The horse cooperated, probably because I was a kid. I would lead the horse over to the gate and climb up to install the harness. Of course, sometimes I had help.

Farm life was not easy but it was a family project. I learned a lot by being involved. Hey, we also had lots of fun. Ole' Prince, one of our work horses, would let us ride him, but if the rider put his heels back in his flanks, he would buck. A close friend, John, and I would see who could ride Prince the most jumps, bareback of course. We also rode the calves.

We are not always called to do easy jobs. Sometimes the Lord calls us to do the difficult ones. Think about a foreign missionary who has to leave loving family members here in the U.S. and go to a foreign culture, learn another language and experience great dangers in order to share God's good news with people who had never heard it. Sometimes we complain when God tells us to do the difficult.

Stop the complaining & go to work! God will equip you and never leave you. He has something great waiting for you when the struggle here has ended. Life here is hardly a blink of the eye compared to eternity. Rejoice that God has selected you to do a special mission for Him! Actually, God has a plan for every believer so, as the great hymn by Annie Coghill says,

> *"Work for the night is coming, Work through the morning hours;*
> *Work while the dew is sparkling; Work 'mid springing flowers:*
> *Work when the day grows brighter; Work in the glowing sun;*
> *Work for the night is coming, When man's work is done."*

2 Timothy 2:15 tells us, *"Do your best to present yourself to God as one approved, a workman who does not need to be ashamed and who correctly handles the word of truth."* God will equip you and strengthen you. You can handle it!

Watermelons Too Good To Sell

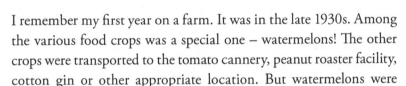

I remember my first year on a farm. It was in the late 1930s. Among the various food crops was a special one – watermelons! The other crops were transported to the tomato cannery, peanut roaster facility, cotton gin or other appropriate location. But watermelons were different.

We planted a patch of melons, but to our surprise a volunteer patch of better melons appeared.

Evidently the previous farmer had let his crop rot in the field and later plowed them under. These melons were large and long, instead of round. We had worlds of melons and would have no trouble selling them.

Dad and Mom were generous people. Dad said watermelons are so good everybody should have some. They were too good to sell. He invited the people at church and others to come and help themselves. When someone would drive to the farm, Dad would fill their trunk with melons.

We are possessors of the greatest message the world has ever received. Everybody should hear it. It's too good to sell. I realize there can be considerable cost involved in radio and television production and that can be relayed to the audience. Yet, we see some ministers (not all, or even most perhaps) who spend much of their time on television begging for funds, promising great financial returns if they give. They do all of this while living in a mansion, owning luxury automobiles and an airplane. I wonder how much of their support comes from people who have a hard time meeting their budgets.

Having such a message, we should be anxious to share it with others. If in a paid ministry position, money should not be among our top decision makers. If your ministry is sincere and reflects the energy for quality work, the people will respond and consider appropriate remuneration. I have never asked for a raise and the people have always responded with a valid salary and expenses in line with what they could reasonably afford.

The Gospel is too good to sell. We must be ready to share it with everyone, in a caring way! Jesus said in John 10:28, *"I give them eternal life, and they shall never perish;"* When Peter and John came across a lame man at the temple gate, Peter said, *"Silver or gold I do not have, but what I have I give you. In the name of Jesus Christ of Nazareth, walk"* (Acts 3:6). In 2 Corinthians 9:7 we are told that *"God loves a cheerful giver."* (Underlines are mine.) Cheerful giving must not apply only regarding material possessions but also our spiritual possession in Jesus Christ. With whom will you freely share today?

My First Car

I was a single freshman at Eastern New Mexico University, having transferred from Oklahoma Baptist University after the first semester. I had grown up mostly in the Portales area and knew lots of people there, so it was more like home. Two other guys and I rented an apartment, rather than staying in a dorm, so I needed a car.

An older acquaintance had a 1938 Chevrolet he wanted to sell. It was about 12 years old but seemed in great shape. I needed to borrow money to finance it, so I went to the bank. Another older friend, D.K., was sure I would need a co-signer so he volunteered. At the bank, Mr. Singleton called me to his desk while D.K. stood over by the wall, waiting to be called when needed. In a brief time the loan papers were prepared and I had signed them without a co-signer. The car, or anything else, did not appear as collateral. Mr. Singleton said, "I know your dad (who now lived in Colorado). The family has always been fully trustworthy and I know you will be faithful in re-paying the loan." D.K. could hardly believe his eyes.

Your reputation follows you and will also impact those with whom you surround yourself. I'm not just talking about business transactions, but in all areas of life. If you will submit to God's direction for your life, He will bless your actions because you are living within His will. Proverbs 31:30-31 says, *"...a woman who fears the LORD is to be praised. Give her the reward she has earned, and let her works bring her praise."* The Father loves His children and watches over them.

Bowling Frustration Away

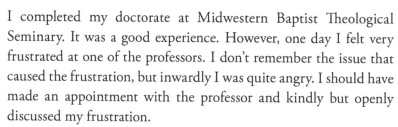

I completed my doctorate at Midwestern Baptist Theological Seminary. It was a good experience. However, one day I felt very frustrated at one of the professors. I don't remember the issue that caused the frustration, but inwardly I was quite angry. I should have made an appointment with the professor and kindly but openly discussed my frustration.

I turned the feelings inwardly instead. Driving back to my living unit, I saw a bowling alley. I am not a bowler and had never bowled a real game.

I knew I needed to externalize my frustration, so I stopped and bowled three or four games. I pretended the pins were the professor and took my anger out by knocking them over. When I had finished, I was  tired and my anguish was gone. The next day I was able to relate to the professor in a normal cheerful mood.

The Bible does not tell us never to get angry, but James 1:19 does tell us to be *"... slow to become angry,"* and in Ephesians 4:26 Paul says, *"In your anger do not sin: Do not let the sun go down while you are still angry."* There are times when we should get angry. Even Jesus got angry sometimes. But, generally, we should address issues in our anger rather than directing it toward persons. God even gets angry at person sometimes, but He knows the total mind and heart of every one; we don't. Just keep in mind the biblical guidelines and act in a caring manner. OK?

The Official Went Down

While a senior in high school, I was fullback on our football team, the Cortez Panthers. This was in the fall and winter of 1948. Cortez is in southwest Colorado and we played teams in Colorado as far away as Grand Junction, and in New Mexico and Utah. I remember a play that occurred in a game in Farmington New Mexico.

The ball was handed off to me. As I came out of the group of would-be tacklers, I floored the linesman and went on for the 50 yard touchdown. I didn't know I had run over an official until the coach mentioned it in school assembly. We won most of our games, but this one was a tie. Back then we did not play overtime.

In preparation for the game of life, both skull practice (study of God's printed word) and contact practice (smaller assignments) are necessary as the Savior equips you for greater things. When working a God-given assignment, keep focused on the goal and put every effort into accomplishing it, following the Coach's directions. There will be obstacles along the way, even some surprises, but the Lord will see you to a successful finish.

Here's a quote from the apostle Paul, found in 1 Corinthians 9:24-27. *"Do you not know that in a race all the runners run, but only one gets the prize? Run in such a way as to get the prize. Everyone who competes in the games goes into strict training. They do it to get a crown that will not last; but we do it to get a crown that will last forever. Therefore I do not run like a man running aimlessly; I do not fight like a man beating the air. No, I beat my body and make it my slave so that after I have preached to others, I myself will not be disqualified for the prize."* Paul is not speaking of earning or losing his salvation based on his works. He has made it clear that his salvation had been permanently given to him through his faith in Jesus Christ. However, he is speaking of the treasures God stores up for us in heaven based on our faithful works. OK, ask the Lord for His assignment and get to work!

She Said, "Yes!"

The Baptist Student Union (BSU) at Eastern New Mexico University would conduct revival meetings, among other things. In 1950, I was asked to take a team and preach a revival, or evangelistic meeting, at a church in Las Vegas, New Mexico, home of the State Teachers' College. I needed a pianist to be one of the team members.

Someone mentioned a girl who was a student at the university on a music scholarship and was active in the BSU. I contacted her and she agreed to go.

She did a great job and the meetings and responses of the people were outstanding. I began to feel that God had arranged this with something in mind for me. Nora and I could be a complimentary team! But I couldn't show my growing attraction for her yet, because that would detract from the work the Lord was doing in connection with the services and visits. It was difficult to wait.

The evening after we had returned to the campus, I invited Nora to go to a popular drugstore for a coke. Back then fountain drinks were served in drug stores. That was a popular gathering place for students. Then we began having real dates, always closing with prayer. If you know you are going to have prayer at the end, you are likely to behave on the date.

About three months later I took Nora on a date to the state park between Portales and Clovis. That evening we parked next to the lake and I asked her to marry me. She said, "Yes," and I was thrilled! We were married March 4, 1951 at the Baptist church of Yeso, New

Mexico. Nora's parents lived at Yeso where her father owned a service station and her mother taught school.

They had provided for a really nice wedding Rev. Alfred Richards, a previous pastor of mine at Calvary Baptist Church in Portales performed the ceremony.

I had been pastor of East Side Baptist Chapel in Tucumcari, New Mexico, a mission of First Baptist Church, and had been driving back and forth from Portales, but by now we had organized the mission into Immanuel Baptist church and a small house had been rented for us.

I probably have included more information than you care to read, but I would like to stress that when your life is yielded to Christ's direction and the guidance of the Holy Spirit, God will arrange for the events and details that fit His plan and your welfare.

Paul's prayer for the church at Philippi, found in Philippians 1:9-11, reveals something to which we should submit: *"And this is my prayer: that your love may abound more and more in knowledge and depth of insight, so that you may be able to discern what is best and may be pure and blameless until the day of Christ, filled with the fruit of righteousness that comes through Jesus Christ not only to believe on Him, but also to suffer for Him,..."*

Again Paul instructs in 2 Timothy 2:15, *"Do your best to present yourself to God as one approved, a workman who does not need to be ashamed and who correctly handles the word of truth."*

God has a plan for every life. Obey His calling and He will shower His blessings on you.

Hospital Orderly, As It Used To Be

In the early 1950's, while attending Eastern New Mexico University, I worked as an orderly at the Roosevelt General Hospital in Portales. In those days, in addition to waxing & buffing floors and making up beds, an orderly did many other things, some not allowed today.

One thing a hospital orderly would do was circulate for surgery. That involved picking up the pads the surgeon had used and tossed on the floor, then hanging them on a rack so they could be counted to make sure none were left in the body.

We would sterilize the needles, and some other items, that had been used. In those days needles were used over & over. Today, a new packaged needle is used each time.

Orderlies sat with patients receiving an IV and with others needing watched. All the orderlies I am aware of during that time were male. We prepared male patients for surgery, and catheterized male patients when needed.

I remember assisting during the setting and penning of broken bones. In fact, on one occasion I administered the anesthesia for the tonsillectomy on a young girl. It was just the doctor and I. However, that was in the days when either was used for simple surgeries such as tonsillectomies. I simply held the either-saturated mask over her nose and mouth and told her to count to ten. Her counting only reached to about seven or eight and had become very slow. The doctor then knew he could begin the surgery.

One day, when a doctor was to perform a cesarean operation, I thought I was going to circulate for the surgery. But the doctor called me to stand with the doctors and nurses around the table. He knew I was a ministerial student and thought this would be meaningful to me. To see the newborn baby pulled from the womb was an experience I will never forget.

I also remember another experience, one I wish I could forget. On this occasion I opened the furnace to put some trash in it. There In the flame I saw the fully formed body of a baby. When I brought the subject up, I was told, "That is the way we dispose of the miscarried fetuses." When God has allowed you the responsibility of caring for a developing baby, I hope you will not cop out and commit murder by abortion. Of course, miscarriages sometimes happen over which you have no control. The one who suffers this kind of loss should not feel guilty because of it.

Oh, did I say we also mopped, waxed and buffed the floors, dusted the room furniture and did other custodial jobs? I don't know why the emergency room was designed to face the west. In the plains of eastern New Mexico we had sand storms from the west. Sometimes one could not even see the house next door and mounds of sand would pile up on the highways. Sometimes it would blast the paint off the exposed side of a car.

On the day of one such storm sand drifted in and piled up in the emergency room to the extent we used a grain shovel to get rid of it. We would tape up all of the windows on the west side, but when such a storm would pass, we would still have to go into the rooms and wipe the sand off of the furniture. I think today, with better land coverage, the results are less drastic.

Did I receive training for any of these jobs? No and yes – none ahead of time but I received on the job training. Some of it included help from others and some simply by experience.

What do you do when, at church, you are asked to serve in a way in which you have no training and feel unprepared? Or, perhaps God has directed your interest toward a particular area of service, but you feel unequipped for the job. Know and accept this: If God instills in you a particular interest, it is for a purpose. He wants to use you in some way related to that interest. If God leads a committee or director to choose you for a task, don't use the excuse, "I could never do that," or "I lack the training." If God calls or selects you, trust Him. He will equip you. There will be someone to guide you when you need assistance, and as for on the job training, the experience will strengthen you.

The wish expressed by the writer of Hebrews for his readers, in 13:21 of that book, is my wish for you: *"May the God of peace, who through the blood of the eternal covenant brought back from the dead our Lord Jesus, that great Shepherd of the sheep, equip you with everything good for doing His will, and may He work in us what is pleasing to Him, through Jesus Christ, to whom be glory forever and ever. Amen."*

Picked Up By a Criminal

In about 1953 I was hitchhiking from a location in south Texas to our home in Portales, New Mexico. Somewhere north of Huntsville a car with one occupant swung over to the side of the highway, knocking my suitcase over, and stopped to give me a ride.

Shortly after we began moving, the driver told me he had just been released from the Huntsville State Prison and the release papers were in the glove compartment. A few miles ahead there was a roadblock and he started looking for a place to detour, but there was none. He was very nervous as we approached the waiting police. However they must have been looking for someone else, as they waived us on. I don't know if the late model car was stolen or not.

After passing the roadblock, the parolee told me he had a job in Houston that he was going to pull and tried to convince me to join him in it. I was glad I had not told him how far I was going. As we approached the next town I told him that this is where I get off and I thanked him for the ride.

In those days there were no cell phones. When I arrived home in Portales, I called the sheriff's department and informed them about what had taken place and gave the best description I could of the car.

Satan is always at work, especially on Christians. He will sneak up on us when least expected and strike us at our weakest point to entice us to join him in his activity. We must always be on guard. You cannot withstand him alone. You must stay in communication with the Savior and let Him empower you.

We are told in 1 Corinthians 10:13 that, *"No temptation has seized you except what is common to man. And God is faithful; He will not let you be tempted beyond what you can bear. But when you are tempted, He will provide a way out so that you can stand up under it."*

Hosting a Homeless
Man Overnight

In the early 1950s, when I was pastor of Immanuel Baptist Church in Tucumcari, New Mexico, I came in contact with a homeless young man who was about 22 or 23 years old. He had no place to stay that night so I introduced him to my wife, Nora, and we invited him to stay with us. We had no spare bed room so, after supper, we fixed him a palate on the floor in the living room.

I kept a baseball bat next to our bed and remained awake much of the night – just in case. This young man had some experience working with cars, so the next day I took him to various garages for possible employment. He was given a job, and after a few days was able to provide for his own housing and food. He came to the church services and within a couple of weeks accepted Jesus as his Savior. I baptized him.

I have passed up many opportunities the Lord has provided me to show others what Christianity is all about, but when I have been faithful the Lord has blessed. It is important that our actions as believers match our message. Sometimes our actions speak as loud, perhaps louder than our words. Is it time for you to take a new look at how consistent your actions match your profession?

James, after declaring that words about commitment are not enough, says in chapter three of his letter, verse 18, *"... Show me your faith without deeds, and I will show you my faith by what I do."*

Jesus says in Matthew 5:16, *"… let you light shine before men, that they may see your good deeds and praise your Father in heaven."* Let God's light shine through you that others will see the way to the Savior.

The Blue Racer Snake

One summer as a teenager I was working for a rancher/farmer in Eastern New Mexico at a place called Milnesand. As you can imagine, it was a place in which there were many heavy sandstorms, but that's another story. The rancher had a son my age and we often worked together and also enjoyed our free time. One day we saw a Blue Racer snake and managed to catch it.

We had the snake with us as we went to the store, the only store for ten miles. The owner of the store saw it and asked if he could release it in his storage building. That was where he stored the extra food items to go on the shelves.

Blue Racers were known to catch mice and he felt this would provide good mouse control. The owner's wife saw the snake and freaked out; she was afraid of snakes. But he released it in the storage area anyway. I wonder if the store owner had a difficult time getting his wife to go get any items from storage after that.

You have a message the world needs do you have the courage to relate it? Perhaps there is the fear of rejection. You may be afraid that others will not only reject the message, but that they will reject you as well.

The reptile is not going to hurt you. If you will rely on the Holy

Spirit and do what He is prompting you to do, the Lord will give you the wisdom, courage and words needed. He will also work on the mind and heart of the one with whom you are sharing.

Peter gives some good advice. In Peter 3:14-15 he says, *"But even if you should suffer for what is right, you are blessed. Do not fear what they fear; do not be frightened. But in your hearts set apart Christ as Lord. Always be prepared to give an answer to everyone who asks you to give a reason for the hope that you have. But do this with gentleness and respect."*

Let this be the start of a new day for you!

The Lord's Perfect Timing

While I was attending Southwest Baptist Theological Seminary in Fort Worth, Texas, I became interim pastor of Fireside Drive Baptist Church in Dallas. An interim serves a pastorless church as it seeks a pastor. Eventually the church called me as its pastor and we needed to move to Dallas. I could drive back to Fort Worth for classes.

It was spring and my neighbor told me that house sales were very slow and ours would not likely sell until in the fall near the time for school to start.

We simply put up a for sale sign in the yard and a small ad in the paper. The next day a family came by. They bought the house and asked me, "What are you going to do with you travel trailer?" I said, "We plan to sell it." They bought the trailer too. The neighbor was flabbergasted.

A few years later our family moved to Maryland where I had accepted the pastorate of First Baptist Church at Kingsville. After six years there I accepted the directorship of two associations and Nora and I were commissioned as home missionaries (now called North American missionaries). We served for twenty years and retired at the end of 1995.

A year after retirement, we wanted to move back to Texas to be near our children and grandchildren. We found a house in Sulphur Springs. A for sale sign had just been put up that day and the ad appeared in the paper. The Harrisons had decided to try to sell it themselves. They needed a month to finish building their new residence. We needed a month to get our house ready to sell. We agreed with the owner on the price, applied for a loan at the bank and returned to Maryland.

We had hardly arrived back to Maryland when the bank called and said, "If you will come on back, we can complete the loan and, I'm sure we can close the sale too." Usually it takes a month or so to close a home sale.

We returned to Sulphur Springs, closed the loan at the bank. The vice president with whom we were working then sent us to the Hopkins County Abstract Office saying, "They may not like it so soon, but they know who butters their toast."

We, along with the owner of the house, met with the Mr. Berry, manager of the abstract office, and agreed on who would be responsible for each item. Then I said, "Don't I need to sign anything?" Mr. Berry said, "No, a handshake is still good in Texas." We agreed on the month for the move and were paid rent for it. All went smoothly.

We had been told that our home in Maryland likely would not sell until spring, or maybe summer. It was December. The realtor conducted an open house. There was a large snowstorm and only two families showed up. One of the families came to the realtor and said, "Would you get those people out of our house." They bought it at the asking price. We never had to return to complete the sale as all was taken care of by FAX.

In each case we had prayed about the move we wished to make and the reason for it. We asked for the Lord's direction and trusted Him with the details. The Lord concluded each deal far quicker than could normally be expected. He even threw in some extra features, assuring us that He was in charge and that we were following His will.

When you are faced with making decisions always consult the Lord and seek His guidance. Be willing to change your plans if He, by the prompting of His Holy Spirit, steers you another way. The Lord will never let you down.

The message the Lord gave to Jeremiah for the people of Judah in captivity also applies to us. In Jeremiah 29:11-13 he says, *"For I know the plans I have for you," declares the Lord, "plans to prosper you and not to harm you, plans to give you hope and a future. Then you will pray to me and I will listen to you. You will seek me and find me when you seek me with all of your heart."* God has a plan for every life. If you will submit to His direction of that plan in your life, He will take care of the timing of important events.

Conversion of an Atheist

When I was pastor of First Baptist Church in Kingsville, Maryland a former atheist who had recently become a believer in Jesus Christ joined the church. He and I often made home visits together. Sometimes, when the conversation became personal, the individual would try to change the subject by asking him a question such as, "Where did Cain get his wife?" They could never get him off course. He would answer, "I don't know anything about that, but I know what Jesus did for me and He can do the same for you."

This former atheist became the head of our bus ministry, picking up children each Sunday, bringing them to church. He later bought a large boat and used it to provide brief refreshing getaways for pastors and their wives.

The truth of 2 Corinthians 5:17-20 was evident in his life. There we find, *"Therefore, if anyone is in Christ, he is a new creation; the old has gone, the new has come! All this is from God, who reconciled us to Himself through Christ, and gave us the ministry of reconciliation: that God was reconciling the world to Himself in Christ, not counting man's sins against them. And He has committed to us the message of reconciliation. We are therefore Christ's ambassadors, as though God were making His appeal through us."*

When a person commits his/her life to Christ, God changes that life and uses it to bless others. How is God using your life? Sometimes a believer needs to make a more complete commitment to the Lord. Are you ready for that? How about right now?

Retired or Retread?

When I retired from my career position in ministry, I did not retire from ministry. The Lord continued to use me as interim pastor and pulpit supply, Bible study leader in rehab and retirement facilities, Sunday school teacher, department director and in other ways. Also, the Lord provides opportunities for day to day personal sharing.

When you retire from your chosen career, God is not through with you. In addition to the mission field of your job environment, He wants to continue using you in ministry to others. This is not limited to career ministers. All believers are called to ministry, during and after employment.

God has gifted you for ministry. This is a lifetime calling. Just as a tire worn smooth can be retreaded for continued service, when you retire from your job, you are given a new field of service. Then when your time on earth is over, the Lord has a great reward for you! For what service has God specially gifted you? How are your gifts being used?

In Romans 5:29 we are told, *"God's gifts and His call are irrevocable."* Paul goes on telling us in 12:6 that *"We have different gifts, according to the grace given us."* He then gives us examples of some of these gifts: prophesying, serving, teaching, encouraging, contributing to the needs of others, leadership, and showing mercy. Paul lists a few additional gifts or callings in Ephesians 4:11, such as evangelist and pastor.

You are no exception. God has also gifted you and called you to use that gift. Do you know what your gift is? If not, search God's printed word; talk to Him and listen for the Holy Spirit to supply you with the answer.

A Website to Reach the World

After retirement as director of missions, the Lord impressed me with the desire to share the gospel in countries where the people have little or no exposure to it. God had equipped me with a computer background and His Holy Spirit urged me to develop a website. I spent a year learning HTML (a computer language) and website dynamics. I wrote the site from scratch in HTML and added some JavaScripts. The site's name was Questgems.com.

This was an extensive, family safe site. In addition to the main menu, there was a contents page providing access to nearly any family-safe subject desired.

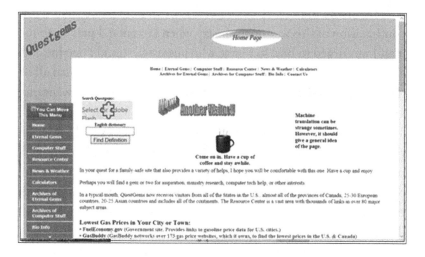

A museum in England asked me to include its link in the Museums section. Lexis automobile wrote asking to have its link included on the purchase section for new autos. You could get the lowest gas prices for your area, constantly automatically updated. Over 1,000 college websites from over the world were linked. Current money exchanges between almost any two countries could be determined. Live cameras were available for various volcanoes and for viewing animals in the jungles. There was a section of ministry helps for pastors and music directors. Computer helps were also available, as well as numerous other features. Except for my updated items, most of these features consisted of links to other sites. I made sure a listed site had no link to any site that would be unsafe for children. Images were used throughout the site.

The main purpose, however, was to draw viewers from all over the world so many of them would be drawn to the Eternal Gems section. There were items explaining the way of salvation and many Christian growth articles, updated monthly. Each month I would get about 100,000 hits (a term used for viewer access) from every state in the US and all but one province in Canada, as well as from every continent and many island nations. I would receive emails from Iran, Iraq, Africa and far eastern countries.

Because of my age, after ten years I became concerned about the continuation of this website ministry when I'm gone. I prayed about it and was urged to find someone who possessed sound doctrine and was equipped to maintain, and contribute to the site. I emailed all of the evangelism directors of the Southern Baptist state conventions and our national agencies.

I made a grave mistake, I prayed about whether I should transfer the site to someone else, but I failed to pray about who I should transfer it to. The person to whom I gave the site worked within one of the convention's evangelism departments. He was not the evangelism director. I interviewed him and was convinced of his doctrinal soundness and had his commitment to keep the site active and properly maintained. So, I gave the site to him, at no cost, forgetting to ask the Lord about it. I just used my judgment. He never updated the site. A little over a year later when I tried to access it there was the notice: "Are you the owner of this site?" Soon the site was completely gone. I later heard, from someone who would know, that Questgems would be an ideal sight for our international missionaries and it had been looked at by those who could have made it available to them. What a big price was paid by my neglecting to consult the Lord on such an important matter.

Don't make my mistake. Stay in tune with the Lord about all matters in life. He may have blessings in store of which you had never dreamed.

Jesus said in Matthew 6:8 that the Father knows what you need before you ask Him. He also said in Matthew 7:7, *"Ask and it will be given you; seek and you will find; knock and the door will be opened to you."* The tense of the verb *"ask"* in the Greek manuscript would indicate a continued or persistent asking. The Lord may test your seriousness in asking, and the purpose must be in accordance with His plan for your life.

Don't make my mistake. Talk to the Lord about your issues and get His direction.

An Unexpected Blessing

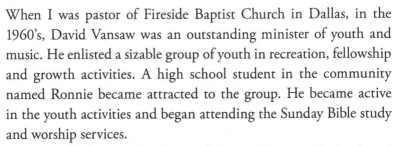

When I was pastor of Fireside Baptist Church in Dallas, in the 1960's, David Vansaw was an outstanding minister of youth and music. He enlisted a sizable group of youth in recreation, fellowship and growth activities. A high school student in the community named Ronnie became attracted to the group. He became active in the youth activities and began attending the Sunday Bible study and worship services.

One Sunday Ronnie accepted Jesus Christ as his Lord and Savior. I baptized him and he began to grow as a Christian. Ronnie became interested in our daughter, Jeannette – so did another young man, but eventually Ron won.

Ron joined the Air Force. We moved to Maryland, but Ron and Jeannette stayed in touch. Eventually Ron Hickey became our son-in-law. He also became a minister of the gospel. While in the USAF he was stationed in the Philippines where Jeannette was able to join him, and later in South Korea.

While in Korea, Jeannette lived with us. After an educational break to complete his college degree, Ron joined the Army in order to continue his work in aviation as he had enjoyed in the Air Force. He worked on airplanes in the Air Force and helicopters in the Army. The Air Force had no current opening in that field. While stationed in the Philippines, Germany and Italy Ron had preaching opportunities. He and Jeannette were able to do missionary work, and develop a puppet ministry.

Since Ron's retiring from the army both he and Jeannette have teaching careers. Ron is also a bi-vocational pastor. Jeannette is an accomplished pianist.

The Lord is good! In addition to Ron and Jeannette being a blessing to so many people, they have been an inspiration and blessing to Nora and me. I want to encourage you to be receptive to the Lord's direction and serve where and how He leads you. He may have some surprises for you, too.

Psalm 107 starts off with *"Give thanks to the Lord, for He is good; His love endures forever."* And we do give thanks. Ron has shown, and continues to show, his love in so many ways!

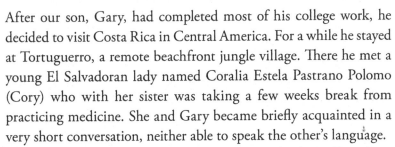

Waiting in El Salvador

After our son, Gary, had completed most of his college work, he decided to visit Costa Rica in Central America. For a while he stayed at Tortuguerro, a remote beachfront jungle village. There he met a young El Salvadoran lady named Coralia Estela Pastrano Polomo (Cory) who with her sister was taking a few weeks break from practicing medicine. She and Gary became briefly acquainted in a very short conversation, neither able to speak the other's language.

At the airport in San Jose when Gary started to leave Costa Rica guess who was standing in the line next to him. It was Cory. They were both surprised and decided to sit next to each other on the flight.

Using a small English/Spanish dictionary, they slowly began to communicate and learned a little about each other. They exchanged mailing addresses as they flew to her home country, El Salvador. Gary continued to Dallas but they kept in touch all year by mail, each having the letters translated for them. During this time her father passed away.

Later Gary returned to El Salvador to meet Cory's family, and on another trip Gary and Cory met in Guadalajara, Mexico where Cory was working. They discussed marriage and later Cory came to the United States on a One Year Fiancée's Visa so they could learn more about each other. An attorney in Gary's church invited her to stay with his family for that time. Gary and Cory became engaged and at the end of the year they were married.

The official ceremony was conducted in the United States, but an elaborate ceremony was also held in El Salvador. Cory had completed her medical degree and soon became a U.S. citizen. Gary later started a forensic laboratory services consulting business and a drug testing service.

Cory is related to a past President of El Salvador. He was in office at a time when El Salvador had good relations with the United States. Gary and Cory were invited to the inauguration and sat in the family section.

Through the ministry of a Southern Baptist missionary Cory and her brother converted from Catholicism to the Christian faith as expressed by Baptists. Gary and Corey have been active members of a Baptist church in Dallas.

The Lord works in mysterious ways sometimes. From an "unlikely" contact He brought two caring people together. They bless our lives. Always be open to God's direction in your life.

Paul's words in 2 Corinthians 2:14 express my feelings of appreciation: *"... thanks be to God who always leads us in triumphal procession in Christ and through us spreads everywhere the fragrance of the knowledge of Him."* This was taking place in the lives of Gary and Cory and in the conversion of Cory and her brother in El Salvador.

A Caring Church

For six years in the 1970's I was pastor of First Baptist Church in Kingsville, Maryland. I had received my Master of Divinity degree at Southwestern Baptist Theological Seminary in Fort Worth, Texas before moving to Maryland, but felt the need for further preparation. I explored the doctoral programs of three of our seminaries. The mini-semesters available at Midwestern Baptist Theological Seminary in Kansas City Missouri seemed to offer the best possibilities, but would this be possible while pastoring a church in Maryland.

The mini-semesters are not a shortcut. For each course students spend all day in one subject area for a month. Nationally recognized guest teachers in the area of study are used in addition to the seminary professor for the course. Later the process would be repeated in another subject area. These mini-semesters would continue until the degree work was completed, including the written dissertation and oral exams.

Prior to each course, about six to eight assigned books must be read and written reviews submitted. While working on the degree we would also be involved in clinical pastoral education in our home area and writing overviews of our counseling sessions. During this time I served as the primary counselor in three of the buildings of the Maryland State Hospital (a mental institution), attending training sessions and regularly reporting to a supervisor.

How would the church react when I share these possible plans? It would require me to be absent from the church a month at a time. I prayed earnestly to the Lord that His will be done and that I would be at peace with the outcome. The church enthusiastically supported the idea. This was a caring congregation!

I met with the deacons and explained that, since this was my idea, I would pay my own transportation and other expenses and I would pay for the supply preachers, but I would trust the deacons to carry on the visitation program during my absence. They said, "No, we (the church) will pay the supply preachers. The church also increased my travel allowance enough to cover my extra mileage. An attender, not a member, presented me with a gift. It was the exact amount, of my tuition. Don't tell me the Lord doesn't watch over His children!

Before my first semester my deacon chairman, Jim Rodgers, said, "That top coat of yours won't stand up to the strong Kansas winds." He insisted I go with him to his tailor to have an adequate top coat custom made for me.

After one of the month long semesters, on my first Sunday morning back, a few of us were in front of the church talking, when this same deacon stopped and said, "I don't like the looks of that tire," pointing to the right rear tire on my car. At first I didn't know what he was talking about. I had forgotten all about the nail puncture I got in a front tire shortly after arriving in Kansas City. I had the tire plugged and moved to a rear location. It happened that the tire was positioned so that by a close look the plug could be seen. Jim insisted that I go with him to his tire dealer and, not just replace the one tire, but get a whole new set of tires, even though the other three were in fine condition. As I noted earlier, this church was filled with caring people.

The doctoral program was new at Midwestern. At my graduation the first such degrees were granted. Since my last name is Brown, I received the first doctoral degree ever conferred by that seminary. While I was gone, the church informally agreed that when I received the degree, they would call me Dr. Brown. Actually, I had rather just be called by my shortened first name, Don, but that is Maryland and I came from Texas. They are more formal in Maryland.

When faced with important decisions in life, earnestly seek the Lord's direction. He is a caring Father who looks after His children. If you follow His direction, He will show His presence every step of the way. Also, when the Lord inspires His people to help you in the process, they will be blessed and their faith will grow.

This church accepted and practiced the words of Jesus who said, *"It is more blessed to give than to receive."* Paul also referred to this statement by Jesus in Acts 20:35. We have a caring Father who watches over His children. 1 John 3:1says, *"How great is the love the Father has lavished on us, that we should be called the children of God!"*

From Handball to Crutches

I recall that several years ago I sprained my right foot playing handball. That foot swelled up about twice the size of the other one. I had just concluded a month long missions engagement in a number of churches in eastern Tennessee. Because  of the sprain, I had to use a crutch when walking and prop my foot on another chair when sitting. My next stop was in Nashville where I had a preaching engagement in one of the churches. It seemed odd, and uncomfortable, using a crutch to approach the pulpit. With the sprained foot not doing its job, the hands, left foot and other parts of my body had to take up the slack.

As painful and uncomfortable the experience was, my hands did not beat on the foot. The other foot, having to bear the whole load, didn't kick the injured foot. Instead, my hands and eyes, and all the body that was able to do so, ministered to the injured member.

In the church, how often do we see the faults of other members & beat them down, rather than helping them up. How often do we get impatient & speak harsh words rather than seeking the good of the church, every member of it. The world sees our faults much quicker than our strengths. I hope you will be one who reaches out with the helping hand.

The apostle Paul said, *"Be completely humble and gentle; be patient, bearing with one another in love. Make every effort to keep the unity of the Spirit through the bond of peace. ... Be kind and compassionate to one another, forgiving each other, just as in Christ God forgave you"* (Eph. 4:2-3, 32).

Helpful Children

The Lord gave us wonderful, caring children in Gary and Jeannette. Then He blessed us with caring spouses for each of them, Ron for Jeannette and Cory for Gary. They all showed special care for their mom and mom-in-law. Gary and Cory live in Dallas, about 75 or 80 miles away. Jeannette and Ron live in southwest Greenville, a distance of about 35-40 miles from our Sulphur Springs home.

When Nora's health was declining she spent times in nursing homes and then at home in a hospital bed. Our children and their spouses, also considered as our children, visited as they could. However, with Jeannette living closer, she would frequently visit her mom after her day of teaching. Ron would come with her sometimes on weekends. Jeannette would liven up her mother's room with such things as balloons with uplifting messages on them and a battery operated dancing dog.

Even since Nora has moved to heaven, both children call me, on alternate days, to be sure I'm O.K. and Jeannette visits me two or three times a week. It's a real blessing to have such caring children.

If you have a parent, family member or friend with special need, consider showing special care. It will brighten up his/her life and you will be greatly blessed.

The apostle Paul said, *"Be imitators of God, therefore, as dearly loved children and live a life of love, just as Christ loved us and gave Himself up for us as a fragrant offering and sacrifice to God"* (Eph 5:1-2).

Procrastination—I Did It

While working on my Doctor of Ministry degree in the late 1970s, I completed a project called "Creative Lord's Supper Services." It included biblical, historical and theological rationales, twelve creative Lord's Supper services and evaluation results from the participants of the various churches that also conducted the services, 224 pages in a hard-back binding.

I had hoped to re-work the document, except for the evaluations, and provide image illustrations for publication. In fact, I received a letter from a pastor in Virginia who had seen the work in the library of Midwestern Baptist Theological Seminary, and he urged me to have it published.

Procrastination is a bad word. I was so busy in meetings and ministry that I thought, "I don't have time right now, but I'm going to do it." The longer I waited the farther the thought went from my mind. Thirty years later I thought I would update and publish the work. However, the various video methods that were popular in the 1970s, movie film projectors, slide projectors, overhead units, tape recorders, etc., were now obsolete. I would need to update some of the methods and locate the material for each. Many other supportive aids do not go out of style. My sermons and services often involved more than the traditional. But I still have not pulled it all together.

As I said, procrastination is a bad word. I am now 88 years old, still preaching when the opportunity is presented and directing an adult Sunday school department, but I don't know if I'm up to all the research for appropriate materials to include. I know – Excuses!

Do you ever procrastinate? You and I need to work on this. Remember the expression, "Don't put off 'til tomorrow what you can do today"? Let's you and I ask the Lord to help us do a better job of attending to business.

Colossians 3:23 tells us, *"Whatever you do, work at it with all your heart, as working for the Lord, not for men."* This instruction directed at some in the church who were slaves, is also appropriate for us. After Peter, in 1 Peter 1:13, told his readers about the action of the prophets that brought Christ's message to them, he said, *"Therefore, prepare your minds for action."* OK, let's do it!

Men, Women and Sinner Sections

One summer in the 1960s I did some summer mission work in east Tennessee. This included various activities including vacation Bible schools and preaching engagements. In one rural mountain church a laymen served as pastoral leader. Every fifth Sunday the pastor of a church in the county seat town would preach for them in an afternoon service. I preached at that county seat church on a fifth Sunday and accompanied the pastor and his wife to the mountain church.

Here is a description of the mountain church's place of worship. It was a small white building, typical of many other small churches. Inside there were three distinct seating sections. Up front and to the right of the pulpit, facing the pulpit, was the men's section. On the other side of the pulpit with the same type of arrangement was the women's section. The sinners' section was in front of the speaker. A pot-bellied stove was in the middle, between the speaker and the sinner's section. Everyone seemed to know where they were to sit and evidently were comfortable with it. All but one, that is.

The pastor had recently married. This was her first visit to the church. When it was near time for the service to start, she took a seat – in the men's section. It was fun watching the men. One would start to sit down, then remain standing, uncomfortably moving around. Finally, she saw the women sitting on the other side and decided to join them. Now all were ready for the service to begin.

Are you sometimes in a situation where you seemed to be "out of pocket"? You weren't sure what to do or how to fit in? What do you do? It may be a company business gathering with a "happy hour" preceding the meeting session.

When I was in the pharmaceutical business in the early 1960s, sometimes there would be gatherings of executives with other companies. Alcoholic drinks would be available during the social period, and most participated. At first I was quite uncomfortable. I saw a soft drink and chose it. But that didn't quite seem right. No one would know that I did not have an alcoholic drink. It is important that we do not dilute our witness with questionable actions. After that first occasion, I would simply not pick up a drink, but freely engage in the conversations.

What would you do in such situations? Perhaps the instruction in Galatians 6:4 will be helpful. Here is Paul's advice, *"Each one should test his own actions. Then he can take pride in himself, without comparing himself with someone else, for each one should carry his own load."*

A Million More in '54

In 1954 Southern Baptists had the slogan, "A Million More in '54." I turned 24 that year and was pastor of First Baptist Church in Santa Rosa, New Mexico. So many churches bought into that theme that Southern Baptists had more additions than ever before. Many were first time believers.

In connection with our theme for the year, our denomination conducted a week long Sunday school conference in California. Churches in the general Los Angeles area hosted the individual sessions. My wife, Nora, and I decided to go.

One of the conference sessions was held at Calvary Baptist Church in El Monte where Dr. Edmond Walker was pastor. Several years later he became executive director of the Hawaii Baptist Convention. In connection with the conference, we conducted a door-to-door religious survey of a residential section of the city. Sometimes the doors were closed as soon as it was learned we represented a church organization. That was quite different from the receptions we were used to in New Mexico.

A session of the conference was led by Hooper Dilday, Training Union director for the Baptist General Convention of Texas. He made a statement that I have remembered through the years. It is, "You do not have to finish the lesson. You are teaching people, not lessons." Sometimes a need surfaces within the class. Addressing the need is more important than completing the lesson prepared. Also, unless an urgent need has risen, dismiss on time. People stop listening and progress already made is sometimes lost if you continue.

Sometimes we think of all the time and effort we have put into research and preparation of a lesson or sermon and feel shortchanged if we can't use it all. But going over time when people are looking at their watches does not help.

The apostle Paul says in Philippians 2:3-4, *"Do nothing out of selfish ambition or vain conceit, but in humility consider others better than yourselves. Each of you should look not only at your own interests, but also to the interests of others."*

The Hawaiian Experience

Nora and I made our first trip to Hawaii on our 25th wedding anniversary. Our children Gary and Jeannette and their spouses Ron and Cory provided us with another one for our 50th anniversary. Each trip provided outstanding experiences.

I'll lump the experiences together as if it all happened on one excursion. Both trips were to Honolulu on the island of Oahu. We were told that when waiting for a bus, if it did not show up at the scheduled time, just relax and wait. It will get there in a little while. "We go by slow time here."

Some businesses and even a bank were wide open so customers did not have a door to open. They could just walk right in. Another impression was the sidewalk shops, even late at night. Also, racks along some of the sidewalks contained coupons for discounts at various restaurants. Speaking of restaurants, I remember a large one that was open to the outside without any doors. Birds would walk around inside, perhaps next to the table where we were eating, but they were calm, didn't fly and did not seem to cause any trouble. I suppose customers kept them well fed.

I had made some wooden items, such as we had used in building relationships in other parts of the world. One day we stopped at a sidewalk shop where we had met a friendly Christian lady the day before. Nora saw and bought a beautiful pink coral bracelet or ring. I don't remember which. We happened to have with us one of the wooden items I had made. We gave it to her. The next night we were walking in the same area. The lady where Nora had made the purchase saw us and called us over. She gave Nora a set of earrings that perfectly matched her purchase the day before. Nora said, "You can't afford to do this." The lady said. "I have had a good day and I want you to have them." All of our experiences were good.

Nora generally preferred to avoid the water, but I decided to learn how to scuba dive. For an hour or two one day I went through the basics in an Olympic sized pool. There I learned to propel myself and how to let any water out that might have gotten into the mask.

The next day I was taken, along with three experienced divers, on a boat out into the ocean. The boat captain and I went down about 30 feet for close to 40 minutes while the experienced divers went to explore an army vehicle that had been destroyed on a ship during WW2, if they could make it that deep.

The water off Hawaii is extremely clear. It is amazing how far one can see. There were beautiful fish of all colors and designs. There was a beautiful coral ridge next to our location. At one point, the captain got behind a large piece of coral and motioned to me to look. He pulled the stone back and a large squid emerged and put out an ink cloud that blocked the view to anything. However, after a few seconds the cloud disappeared and the water was as clear as before. This was a defense mechanism for the squid. An attacker would not know where to attack and the squid would have time to escape. After re-boarding the boat, we moved closer to the site of the other divers and picked them up. One of them had not been able to go quite deep enough to examine the sunken vehicle. The pressure caused too much pain. This was one of the outstanding experiences of my life.

Dr. Edmond Walker was executive director of the Baptist Convention of Hawaii. Nora and I had become acquainted with him in 1954 when we attended a Sunday school conference in El Monte, California. Part of the conference was conducted in the church of which he was pastor. While we were in Hawaii we decided to go by his office and say hello to him. To our pleasant surprise, Edmond wanted to take us on a tour of Baptist work in Hawaii. He showed and told us about some of the works in progress and included a tour of the Baptist college in Honolulu. The whole Hawaiian experience was educational and enjoyable.

The Lord has made a beautiful world. To explore it can be a worshipful experience. The psalmist, in the 148th Psalm was caught up in praise to God for His creation, as though the created objects themselves should, praise the Lord. He says, *"Praise the Lord. ...Praise Him, sun and moon, praise Him all you shining stars. Praise Him you highest heavens and you waters above the skies. Let them praise the name of the Lord, for He commanded and they were created. He set them in place forever and ever; He gave a decree that will never pass away. Praise the Lord from the earth, you great sea creatures and all ocean depths, lightning and hail, snow and clouds, stormy winds that do His bidding, you mountains and all you hills, wild animals and all cattle, small creatures and flying birds, ..."* As we travel, let us enjoy God's creation and praise Him!

Encouragement can also be received as we share with others and others share with us about how He is using our efforts to reach and disciple people, as took place between Edmond Walker and us. Don't be bashful – Share!

Say, "Nothing at All"

A humorous experience occurred in east Tennessee on a Saturday night following the service of a county-wide evangelism crusade. The services were held in the high school gymnasium and led by the state Baptist convention's evangelism director. That Saturday night I had been invited to give my testimony and the next morning to preach at a church in another city.

After the Saturday night service, two other workers and I were riding with the pastor of the church to where we would spend the night. I would be preaching at his church the next morning. The pastor told us how difficult it was for him to tell a humorous imaginative story, because the congregation would think he was serious, and he would have to go back and explain it.

I remembered seeing a cemetery that was about a mile off the highway to where we were going. I told the pastor about the location of the cemetery and said, "At that cemetery there is an Indian grave. You can go up to that grave and say, 'What are you doing here, Mr. Indian?' and he will say, 'Nothing at all.'" The pastor said, "Really? That's hard to believe." I said, "It won't take you long to find out." One of the other workers was a very brilliant and alert person and caught on to what was going on. He gave some encyclopedic explanation that made it sound plausible.

The pastor said, "It is near midnight and people here shoot first and ask questions later." I said, "OK, if you don't want to know." His curiosity got the best of him. He turned off the highway and drove down to the cemetery. I showed him a grave about midway on the first row and said, "Here is the Indian man's grave." The pastor went over to the grave and said, "What are you doing here Mr. Indian?" All was quiet. I said, "You spoke pretty softly. He probably couldn't hear you." The pastor raised his voice and repeated the question. All was silent. I said, "He is six feet under. It will take some volume for him to hear." The pastor, with a rather loud voice asked the question again. Then he said, "He didn't say anything." I said, "I told you he would say nothing at all and we had to go two miles out of the way at midnight just to prove it. But don't worry, I won't tell you congregation."

I wouldn't pull this on just any pastor, but I had learned that he had a good sense of humor and often pulled jokes on people.

The Christian life doesn't have to be boring. Some Christians walk around, or even sing in the choir, with expressions on their faces that look like they have lost their last friend. They look unhappy. We have much to be happy about! If you start looking happy, you might start feeling happy. Let's reflect the joy that is available in the Christ life!

The 47th Psalm should give your heart a lift. Here are the first few verses of it: *"Clap your hands, all you nations; shout to God with cries of joy. How awesome is the Lord Most High, the great King over all the earth! … God has ascended amid shouts of joy, the Lord amid the sounding of trumpets. Sing praises to God, sing praises; sing praises to our King, sing praises."*

After Jesus told His disciples that He was the vine and they were the branches and that they should love one another as He had loved them, He said, in John 15:11 *"I have told you this so that my joy may be in you and that your joy may be complete."*

Florida Disaster

Hurricane Andrew struck Florida in August 1992. It was a category 5 with winds up to 165 mph and was the most destructive storm Florida had experienced up until that time. It destroyed 63,500 homes and damaged 124,000 others, stripping many homes of everything but their concrete foundations.

I was the director of missions for Blue Ridge and Central Baptist Associations in Maryland at the time. The directors of missions across the state decided to go as a team to assist in relief for a week. We received the training and the credentials provided by the state convention in accordance with the directions supplied by the Southern Baptist Disaster Relief in partnership with FEMA, the Department of Homeland Security and we committed to 12 hour days.

We, and many other volunteers, slept in one of the large tents on the parking lot of one of the churches. Lumber yards and hardware stores over the U.S. shipped supplies which were stacked and stored on that lot as well. In fact, one night a heavy rain forced the top of the tent in which we were sleeping to sag so low with a heavy load of water on it that we had to move to keep from being crushed in the collapse. Part of the church building was opened up for us to sleep in for the remainder of the week.

During the week we did roofing, drywall and other repairs. We formed a variety of teams. The team I was on first did some repairs for a Catholic family. At the completion, the family provided a large meal for us and asked us about our beliefs and how they differed from theirs. They listened intently and expressed their thanks.

Next we did roofing, construction and drywall for a Hindu family. This family had a shrine in their back yard. They were originally from India but had lived several years in Columbia. It was from there that they had immigrated and were now American citizens.

Earlier, someone posing as a building contractor had sized up their needs and in the process learned what they had in savings. The payment was required in advance. He promised they would begin the work on the following Monday. Neither he nor anyone else showed up to work. The man from India, let's call him Akbar, after relating what had happened, said, "You Christians, you Baptists, came and did all the work and even supplied the materials. You didn't charge anything!" Akbar and his wife, we'll call her Nikhla, prepared a large Indian meal for us.

I had a number of opportunities to sit down and visit with Akbar. Two weeks prior to the hurricane, Akbar's and Nikhla's son had died in a boating accident. They thought one of the gods was punishing them because they had cut down a particular tree in the back yard.

In so many religions, other than Christianity, it is thought that the gods hold the people as slaves and when they displease a god they can expect to be punished. I was able to share with Akbar about a God who loves him so much, He even sacrificed His Son to provide him a full and meaningful life on earth and when his time on earth is over God wishes to take him home to His house in heaven for all eternity. God's perfect Son, Jesus, was willing to die on a cross, and carry Akbar's sins to the grave. To experience this he must ask God to forgive all of his sins, accept God's great sacrifice and yield to God's lordship of his life. God the Father raised Jesus His Son from the grave to live again. And many people later even witnessed

His ascension into heaven. And by trusting Jesus Christ as Savior we can live with Him eternally.

Akbar seemed under conviction but never made the commitment. However, God prepared for the follow-up. Akbar's best friend lived across the street. He was a Latin American with Spanish as his first language. Akbar was fluent in Spanish, having lived in Columbia so long. His friend was a deacon in a Baptist church and was a solid Christian. I was able to share with him about Akbar and he would follow-up.

The apostle reminds us that God sometimes uses multiple people to bring a person to Christ. He compares it to raising a crop. Paul says, in 1 Corinthians 3:6, *"I planted the seed, Apollos watered it, but God made it grow. So neither he who plants, nor he who waters is anything, but only God who makes things grow. The man who plants and the man who waters have one purpose, and each will be rewarded according to his own labor. For we are God's fellow workers..."*

Jesus himself told us, *"All authority in heaven and on earth has been given to me. Therefore go and make disciples of all nations ..."* (Matthew 28:16-19).

In the original language, the verb *"go"* can be translated "as you go" The phrase *"make disciples"* is a command. Jesus has commanded every Christian to make disciples. We also are to be involved in, or supporting, the baptism and developing of those new disciples. The rest of the above passage will affirm that.

The workplace may be your field for disciple-making. You're retired? Get out of that easy chair and ask the Lord to guide you to someone who needs God's good news. Even a student has the whole school as a mission field. Perhaps God is calling you to a full time ministry here or somewhere else in the world. Whatever you do, you cannot make disciples under your own power. You must let God's Holy Spirit work through you. He will teach you what to say and how to say it, as well as when and how to listen. Sometimes you can only plant the seed. At other times you will be able to reap the crop as God brings it to fruition.

Alright! What are you waiting for?

Spring Break in Rhode Island

What does the phrase "Spring Break" bring to mind? The time when some high school and college students head for the beach? Simply a break from studies and perhaps a family vacation? Well, seminaries have spring breaks too. It gives willing students an opportunity to engage in special ministries. I'd like to tell you about one of my spring breaks.

This, I believe was in the spring of 1967. Three of us, students at Southwestern Baptist Theological Seminary, went to Rhode Island which is the smallest state in the US. I was the evangelist for a revival meeting at a church in Newport, next to the Naval Station in which was located the Naval War College and the Naval Justice School. One of our team members was the song leader and all three of us were involved in a door-to-door religious survey in nearby Somerset, Massachusetts where a new church was being started.

Most of those attending the services were either stationed at the naval base or were civilian workers at the base, and their families. I do not remember the number of decisions, but most of those attending were committed Christians, so most of the decisions would be in the form of re-commitment, a step of growth in their Christian walk.

Our noon meals each day were in the Officers' Mess Hall. We also were treated to a tour of a submarine that was in port. A hall leading through part of the sub was arranged so that after each short distance there would be a 90° turn and a coffee pot in a recessed area. The Naval officer guiding us would stop and make cleanliness inspections with white gloves at each of these recessed areas. At one of the coffee pot locations, the officer said, "The Navy lives on two things, ayl and coffee and sometimes we think we can get by without the ayl" (his pronunciation of oil).

Opportunities for service abound. If you will ask Him, the Lord will open doors in line with your gifts and His plan for your life. As you submit to His calling and respond to His leading you may be surprised with the additional adventures the Lord provides you.

Jesus said in Luke 11:9, *"Ask and it will be given you; seek and you will find; knock and the door will be opened to you."* If you have been wondering how to engage in a ministry in line with your gifts, do what Jesus said. Ask Him! If you are sincere, He will show you and open a door for service.

We Go After Hugo

On September 22, 1989 South Carolina and the lower east coastal areas suffered America's most destructive hurricane up until that time. According to Wikipedia.org this storm "caused 34 fatalities (mostly by electrocution or drowning) in the Caribbean and 27 in South Carolina, left nearly 100,000 homeless, and resulted in $10 billion (1989 USD) in damage overall."

Blue Ridge and Central Baptist Associations, in the Baptist Convention of Maryland/Delaware, were the two associations I directed. We decided to assist in supplying many of the urgent needs of which the Red Cross had made us aware. After supplies had been collected from the churches, the vehicles and drivers met very early one morning at South End Baptist Church in Frederick, Maryland. We formed a caravan and headed for Charleston South Carolina where we would receive information and general instructions.

A trucking firm in Hagerstown heard about what we were planning and informed me that they had been saving up sleeping cots for such an occasion and would like to participate in the  effort. A large Baptist church in Charleston had provided a sizable space as a temporary shelter. They were happy to receive the large number of cots delivered by the trucking firm.

After arriving in Charleston and receiving instructions, our team dispersed into various areas. We were in some of the towns before the Red Cross or any kind of assistance had appeared. Electric lines were on the ground, houses were greatly damaged and trees were uprooted or broken off. In one town the mayor and a number of people had gathered in a building. We had baby diapers, food items, clothing and other things that we had been informed were needed. The mayor said, "You are the first people we have seen who have come to help." We unloaded a van of supplies and the people indicated that these were greatly needed and they expressed their appreciation.

We returned home on cloud nine. We had seen the need and felt the expressed appreciation of the people. It touched us deeply. I have noticed, on this and other mission trips, that after returning home we felt that we were the ones most blessed.

Have you had this experience? If not, I'm sure there are opportunities around you with people in need. For some it might be labor that's needed, such as mowing the lawn or volunteering to cook for someone who is sick or injured, or supplying food or other necessity for a family that has temporarily lost their income. There are opportunities for volunteering at the hospital, senior center or with a charity group. Your church may be involved in mission trips, or may need help within its own organization. It doesn't matter if you are a teenager, young or median adult or a senior citizen. There are places or ways for making a contribution. Parents, I hope you are showing your children how they can contribute in a meaningful way. They learn both by example and by doing.

The psalmist in 41:1 says, *"Blessed is he who has regard for the weak."* Jesus said that it is more blessed to give than to receive. He took on the role of a servant and washed His disciples' feet, dirty from walking the dusty trails in their sandals. Also in John10:28 Jesus draws the picture of Him being the Shepherd and us as His sheep. There He says, *"I give them eternal life."* He did this at a great cost, even hanging on the cross and shedding His blood for us.

Is the cost too great for you to reach out to others in need, whether it is a physical or spiritual need, or both? Now is a good time to start!

Katrina in New Orleans

Hurricane Katrina slammed into New Orleans on August 29, 2005. The center of the storm passed southeast of the downtown area, striking St. Bernard and Plaquemines parishes.

However, the hurricane force winds downtown and in the residential areas caused enormous damage and loss of life. According to Wikipedia.org, "The failures of levees and floodwalls during Katrina are considered by experts to be the worst engineering disaster in the history of the United States. By August 31, 2005, 80% of New Orleans was flooded, with some parts under 15 feet (4.6 m) of water. ...Between 80 and 90 percent of the residents of New Orleans were evacuated before the hurricane struck." Wikipedia also stated that "According to a modeling exercise conducted by the U.S. Army Corps of Engineers (USACE), two-thirds of the deaths in Greater New Orleans were due to levee and floodwall failure."

First Baptist Church of Sulphur Springs, Texas was one of the early responders. I had the privilege of being included in one of those groups.

Our teams were involved in everything from cleanup, re-construction, and food distribution. The Celebration Church provided a very large space in its facility, divided into men's and women's sections, for housing our teams and many others from over the United States. FBC in Sulphur Springs has continued to send recovery groups for at least 12 years after the hurricane.

A large commercial fishing boat was sitting in the street of a housing development. We were told by the owner that the hurricane had lifted it from the water, over the trees and deposited it at that location.

The houses had all been searched for people, dead or alive. Those containing one or more dead persons were marked on the outside, so the persons charged with their recovery would know where to go.

As we reached out to help those who had come back to the area, they would give us a big bear-hug and share with us how we could pray for them. We returned to Sulphur Springs feeling that we had received the greater blessing. It feels good to help someone in need! And it pleases God!

Are you reaching out to others, or are you focused only on your own needs? The Lord will help you to re-focus. Or, have you made Jesus the Lord of your life? Jesus said in Luke 15:7 that there would be great rejoicing in heaven over one sinner who repents. Jesus gave His life so that when one repents and submits to His Lordship, that person will receive a new life in the here and now and eternal life with Him. The writer of Hebrews tells us, in chapter 12, verse 2, *"Let us fix our eyes on Jesus, the author and perfecter of our faith, who for the joy set before Him endured the cross, scorning its shame, and sat down at the right hand of the throne of God"* (Underline mine). Does this speak to your need?

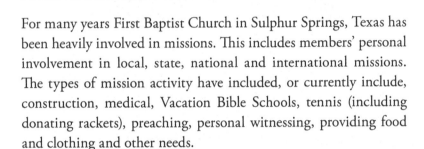

Missions in Milwaukee

For many years First Baptist Church in Sulphur Springs, Texas has been heavily involved in missions. This includes members' personal involvement in local, state, national and international missions. The types of mission activity have included, or currently include, construction, medical, Vacation Bible Schools, tennis (including donating rackets), preaching, personal witnessing, providing food and clothing and other needs.

In early 1997 I arrived on the scene and learned that pastor Dr. David Hardage, who is now executive director of the Baptist Convention of Texas, had a missions heart and had led the church to reach out beyond itself.

I had the privilege of going on the first three mission trips to Milwaukee, Wisconsin.

We reconstructed the interior of the Baptist associational office there, did extensive interior work on an intercity church and re-roofed a church building. Some of the group conducted VBS and a tennis camp in which the gospel was presented. Pastor Hardage led the trips in which I participated and worked alongside us. Coach Mike Anderson headed the tennis project in a city near Milwaukee. Often after a hard day's work we looked forward to the trip to a popular frozen custard location. In the picture, Pastor David Hardage is sitting on the end of the bench and I am standing next to the pole.

Has the Lord spoken to you regarding your involvement in missions outreach? If you are a pastor, are you leading your church to reach beyond itself? A church that is not involved in some kinds of ministry beyond itself tends to look inward and see its differences which can lead to breaks in relationships and reduced effectiveness. A church extending its ministry beyond itself sees its togetherness in reaching out. Differences are minimized and unity is strengthened.

Jesus said in Matthew 6:19-21, *"Do not store up for yourselves treasures on earth, where moth and rust destroy, and where thieves break in and steal. But store up for yourselves treasures in heaven, where moth and rust do not destroy, and where thieves do not break in and steal. For where your treasure is, there your heart will be also."*

Our Lord also told His disciples, *"The harvest is plentiful but the workers are few. Ask the Lord of the harvest, therefore, to send out workers into His harvest field"* (Matthew 9:37). When you sincerely pray with this request, The Lord may say, "You are one of the workers I have selected," and show you the field in which He wants you to work. Get with it!

Missions Are Local Too

There are needs all around us. An elderly person's house may need painting, but he or she is not able and does not possess the funds to have it done. Perhaps someone's water or drain system needs minor plumbing but the ability and funds are not available. A light bulb needs replaced, but it is unsafe for the disabled or older person to get on a stepladder for the task.

The church as a whole, or you as an individual, can show your care by addressing common needs of people around you. First Baptist Church in Sulphur Springs, Texas addresses those needs. In addition to what is commonly thought of as local mission projects, the church has a care group of volunteers. This group meets and discusses surfaced needs and prays for those involved. They also get personally involved and everything is kept confidential. Not even the names of the volunteers are given.

When I needed to have a day procedure at the hospital, and my wife was bed-ridden, a man on the care group called and volunteered to transport me to and from the hospital as well as wait there until I was dismissed to go home. I would like to give his name, and could, but they do not publicize their actions.

A Sunday school class or department also needs to reach beyond itself. When I was teacher of a class at FBC, we had several projects. We re-finished the interior of a small church in a nearby community, painted the deteriorating exterior trim of a widow's house and raked the leaves for an elderly couple, among other things. This was a class of senior adult men. Other classes were, and are, also involved in projects. A lady's class has made lap quilts for nursing home residents. On an individual basis my wife Nora has made stuffed teddy bears for children, as well as quilts designed and sized for children and given them to a home for abused women, among other things. After she was bedridden, she would take the church's prayer list and the prayer concerns of her class and pray for them daily.

Whatever your situation may be, there are caring actions available to you. If you wear the name of Christian, then your actions should be consistent with your profession. Jesus Christ set the example for us and told us to do likewise. In Matthew 10:8 Jesus instructs, *"… Freely you have received, freely give."* He also said, as we find in Luke 6:38, *"Give, and it will be given to you. A good measure, pressed down, shaken together and running over, will be poured into your lap."* In Acts 20:35 Paul reminds us of Christ's words when He said, *"It is more blessed to give than to receive."* After all, Christ gave His life for us. Look around you. Where do you need to give – whether energy, goods or money?

Dachau

When our son-in-law, Ron, was stationed in Germany Nora and I went to see him, our daughter Jeannette and our grandchildren, Joshua and Jessica. As mentioned in another experience, they took us on some tours in southern Germany, as well as an extended trip including Switzerland, Liechtenstein, Austria and the Netherlands.

One stop was a very sobering one. It was the Dachau death camp, located near Munich. The following is based upon information found on the Internet at https://www.history.com/topics/world-war-ii/dachau.

Hitler established the camp shortly after he became chancellor of Germany in 1933. It initially was for political prisoners, but later became a death camp for his effort to exterminate Jews. Thousands died from starvation, overwork, or execution. Some of the prisoners were subjected to brutal medical experiments. One such experiment was "to determine the feasibility of reviving individuals immersed in freezing water. For hours at a time, prisoners were forcibly submerged in tanks filled with ice water. Some prisoners died in the process."

The camp also included other groups Hitler considered unfit for the new Germany. Over 30,000 Jews were sent to the concentration camps at Dachau, Buchenwald and Sachsenhausen, 11,000 of them at Dachau. One source said that Dachau was built to house 6,000, but its population grew to about 30,000.

The U.S. military rescued those at Dachau on April 29, 1945. It is said that over 200,000 prisoners were registered as passing through the gates at Dachau, but thousands were never registered, making it impossible to know the exact number imprisoned or died there.

A memorial site was created at the Dachau site in1965. When we were there we were able to tour its historic buildings. There are also special exhibits and a library relating to the camps sad history. The visit was not exciting. It was a downer, but important for us to know the extent to which Jews and some others were treated by a ruthless, wicked dictator.

What about today? Do we have hate groups, or individuals, who think those of some races or cultures are less valuable and perhaps should be exterminated? God does not make that kind of distinction. He sacrificed His Son for all people. Jesus said in John 12:32, *"But I, when I am lifted up from the earth, will dray all men to myself."* The drawing power is there, but not everyone will let go of the world and yield to His drawing power. John 3:16 tells us that because God loves the whole world, He sacrificed His Son for everybody. All you need to do is let go of the world and let Him take charge of your life.

Pioneer Crossing

In Sulphur Springs, Texas there is a development of beautiful apartments for senior citizens called Pioneer Crossing. It is not connected with a rehab center. These are beautiful duplex apartments. Each apartment has its own garage. These apartments encircle a nice swimming pool. These are purchased by the residents for $100.00 down.

At the entrance to this site is the administration building. Inside, beside the business office, there is a roomy area for meetings or visiting. Free coffee is available. It leaves a comfortable atmosphere.

The senior adult pastor of First Baptist Church, Fred Lewis, began a Bible study in the roomy area of the administration building. Then he enlisted Bible study leaders for this location, as he does for the health and rehab centers. I have had the privilege of leading the Bible studies at Pioneer Crossing, as has another person or two. Those attending are eager to learn and participate in the studies and these people become close friends. It is a great joy to be involved.

This is a type of ministry in which a lay member of the church can participate. Perhaps you have felt ill-equipped for some types of mission trips or other ministries. This kind of Bible study ministry, or one in a health and rehab center, often called a nursing home, may be right down you alley. Your personal Bible study will be sufficient for sharing in these locations. Professional study in a Bible college or seminary is not required. Give it some thought and ask for the Lord's direction.

We are told in Romans 12:11, *"Never be lacking in zeal, but keep your spiritual fervor, serving the Lord."* Jesus told His disciples, in John 9:4, *"As long as it is day, we must do the work of Him who sent me. Night is coming when no one can work."* Today, this applies to us, His disciples. Are you one of Christ's disciples? Then get to work!

God Said, "Go to Whataburger."

After retiring as director of missions for two associations in Maryland, Nora and I moved to Sulphur Springs, Texas in order to be near our kids and grandkids. One day I was pondering about how to develop relationships with non-Christian or unchurched men in order to minister to them. I had not grown up or gone to school in the area so did not know many local people.

I started praying about the situation. I got the strongest feeling that I needed to go to Whataburger, a local fast food place. I shared this with Nora and said, "The urge is so strong I believe God is telling me to go to Whataburger. I don't really understand it, but I'm going." It was about 3:30 in the afternoon. I picked up a computer magazine to read and left.

At Whataburger I found an empty table and sat down with a cup of coffee and my magazine. In a little while a man came and sat at the large round table next to mine. We started talking and I discovered he was a member of a church and attended most of the time. Another man came and sat at the round table. He also was involved in a church. The same was true of the third man. I began to wander what the urge was all about. Perhaps I had misunderstood. The men invited me to join them. They met daily just for coffee, fellowship and to catch up on all the area news. Then a forth man came and sat down. This is why I was there.

I'll call him Boyce. Boyce was a morally upright person, but thought that's all God requires. His dad had been a good man and Boyce was sure he was in heaven. I did not find out about all of this in that first meeting and I would not embarrass him before the others. I had a season football pass for two and, as we got to know each other, invited Boyce to a game. He was not interested in going to games, but it seems the very invitation let him know we could be friends.

I found times to talk with Boyce on the days we were the last two to leave the table. I never mentioned anything about his dad's trusting in a "good" life being enough. It would have been painful and serve no positive purpose. Boyce came to understand that we have all sinned and heaven is a holy place where sin cannot enter. But God loved us so much that He sacrificed His Son to provide a complete pardon, cleaning our record. Jesus was willing to suffer, go to the cross, be buried and on the third day come alive again. On one occasion the risen Lord was seen by over 500 people. After 40 days people watched as He ascended to heaven.

Boyce understood that to receive this salvation he must repent of his sin, ask God for forgiveness and ask Jesus to come into his life as Savior and Lord. Boyce did this. A few years later Boyce developed a dementia and died. I was asked to conduct his funeral.

I'd like to share two passages. John 3:16-18 tells us, *"For God so loved the world that He gave his one and only Son, that whoever believes in Him shall not perish but have eternal life. ... Whoever believes in Him is not condemned, but whoever does not believe stands condemned already because he has not believed in the name of God's one and only Son."* In verse 16, the word *"in"* is important. Either of two words in the Greek manuscripts could have been used. One is *"en"* and the other is *"eis."* Both are normally translated "in." However, in the study of the language, the word *"en"* is illustrated as a circle with an arrow going around it. *"Eis"* is illustrated by a circle and an arrow going into it. This is the word used in John 3:16. A more accurate translation would be "Whoever believes into Him is not condemned."

An easier understanding of the difference in the two prepositions above may be this: I could observe a chair. It looks well built and strong. I believe it will hold my weight. That is believing facts about the chair (the circle with an arrow going around it). I sit down in the chair. I have trusted it with my weight. I have believed into it (the circle with an arrow going into it). This is what John 3:16 says. We must believe into (trust) Jesus as Savior.

The other verse I want to share is John 12:32 where Jesus says, *"But I, when I am lifted up from the earth, will draw all men unto myself."* This reminds me of the old horseshoe magnets we as children used to play with. You could hold it over a pile of nails and they would flock to it. However, if you would hold it in front of a nail secured in the wall, that same drawing power is there, but the nail will refuse to let go of the wall. That's the way it is with people. Christ's drawing power is at work, but many people will refuse to let go of the world and come to Him.

What about you? The world or Christ?

Hindu Friend, a Work in Progress

I have a friend who is a Hindu from India. At one time he was owner of a service station in Sulphur Springs, Texas. Nora and I used to eat lunch at the small cafe located in the station. Tushar (not his real name) and I got to know each other well and enjoyed sitting and talking. Tushar has a wife and two elementary aged children. I started out building a relationship, rather than immediately confronting him about his spiritual needs.

On one occasion he returned to India for a week to visit his parents. His father was to have major surgery. Tushar asked me if I would approve any requested help the cafe manager might ask for while he is gone. There were already persons to call on if needed. I agreed to do so.

At another time the city had a local option coming up. Our church was preparing signs to put in yards opposing the sale of alcohol drinks. I mentioned this to him. He said he would like to help and if he could meet with my pastor and me he would appreciate it. We met in the cafe and after a few minutes, he excused himself and briefly went to his office and returned. Tushar had $2,000 in cash and handed it to my pastor to contribute toward the sign effort.

Tushar and family were fluent in English. I asked him to share with me about Hinduism. What do they believe? He had a limited knowledge about it and said his wife was better equipped for this. I shared and discussed my beliefs and talked to him about a God who loved him so much He sacrificed His Son to provide a meaningful life in the here and now and an eternal life in heaven with Him where there is eternal joy. This contrasts with the belief in several gods who hold you as slaves and punish you when slip up. Also, it is a far cry from the belief in returning in a higher or lower form, depending on how you live, hoping eventually to reach nirvana. I also gave Tushar and his wife a tract and a New Testament. I had referred to the Gospel of John, so to make things easier I also gave him a copy of John's gospel.

Later Tushar sold his station in Sulphur Springs and bought one in Mt. Pleasant where he lives. Mt. Pleasant is only about 30 miles away. We still have a good relationship. Tushar has not yet accepted Christ as his Savior. I still hope he will.

Do you get discouraged when a few persons you have witnessed to fail to accept Jesus Christ as Savior? If so, I wish to remind you that you are not responsible for the other person's decision. You are responsible for sharing; the other person is responsible for his or her decision. In Matthew 28:19 you have the command from Jesus himself to make disciples as you go about in this world and in Acts 1:8 he makes it clear that we are to be His witnesses. In Romans 10:14 Paul poses the question, *"How then can they call on the one they have not believed in? And how can they believe in the one of whom they have not heard? And how can they hear without someone preaching to them?"* Just continue to share the good news!

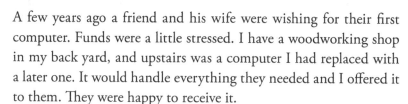

A Fall to Remember

A few years ago a friend and his wife were wishing for their first computer. Funds were a little stressed. I have a woodworking shop in my back yard, and upstairs was a computer I had replaced with a later one. It would handle everything they needed and I offered it to them. They were happy to receive it.

In the shop I have one of those pull down stairs. They are somewhat steeper than conventional stairways. I retrieved the computer monitor and had it in my arms as I started down. The weight out in front of me got me off balance.

The monitor and I fell from near the top of the stairs. I fell across the lawn mower that was nearby and was amazed that neither I nor the computer monitor had any breaks. I got up, thanked the Lord and retrieved the remaining items.

Unexpected events will happen in life. When things turn out well some people will attribute it to their own skills or decisions. When things turn out bad, some will blame God. But God does not promise that we will never experience difficulties, hurts or disappointments. In fact God watches over His children and cares for them. We must take the blame for our failures. God may allow these to happen to remind us that we are not self-sufficient. He may use the incident to teach us a lesson for our own good and to draw us back to a closer relationship with Him.

The apostle Paul went through a lot of hardships and one time he had been stoned and left for dead. But he found in each situation a door opened for sharing the gospel. In Romans 8:18 Paul said, *"I consider our present sufferings are not worth comparing with the glory that will be revealed in us."* Then in verses 28-29 he continues, *"And we know that in all things God works for the good of those who love Him, who have been called according to His purpose. For those God foreknew he also predestined to be conformed to the likeness of His Son..."* And in verse 31 he adds, *"What, then, shall we say in response to this? If God is for us, who can be against us?"*

Name Change, No Go

In the 1975 Sothern Baptist annual convention in Miami Beach, the proposal to change the name of the convention for greater acceptance in non-southern states and countries outside the U.S. was defeated. No specific name had been suggested. A committee was to study the idea and make a recommendation.

If a company executive suggested changing the company name, and was asked for a suggestion, would answer, "I don't know, just change it," I doubt there would be much support. That's basically what had happened at the SBC convention.

I had suggested a name and this had been published in many state Baptist papers. At the convention I was asked to make my recommendation in form of a motion. It was on the last night of the convention with the largest attendance we had ever had. Perhaps this was because it included a celebration of the 50th anniversary of the Cooperative Program, a method for the churches to cooperate in the support of world missions. All other business had been concluded that afternoon.

Since the cooperation of churches was so important for Southern Baptists, I suggested the name "Cooperative Baptist Churches." Technically, we are only a convention when we convene, which is once a year. A well known pastor in the Deep South arose and said, "If they don't like the name "Southern" let them go somewhere else. My motion failed. The record is located at www.baptist2baptist.net/Issues/SBCNameChange/1975Study.asp.

Actually, later I was glad the motion failed, because it was at a time in Southern Baptist history that division was rising rapidly. Cooperation was lacking. The name perhaps would have been a means for ridicule.

However, in August of 1990 a group that broke away from the SBC adopted the name "Cooperative Baptist Fellowship." I am not a part of that denomination, but can't help but wonder if the presentation and discussion that night had any influence on their adopted name.

Life does not always go the way you wish it would. You may have strong convictions and exert your influence in the best way you know, but your organization or community may turn a deaf ear.

If your intentions are God-honoring and you have prayed about you actions, the Lord will take notice and may surprise you by His actions. Your influence does not die. He may put your idea and motivation in the hearts and minds of others.

When Paul was in prison in Rome, he spoke to a group of religious people who had a background that should have affirmed his message to them. In Acts 28:23-25 we find that *"from morning till evening he explained and declared to them the kingdom of God and tried to convince them about Jesus from the Law and from the Prophets."* Even with Paul's conviction and effort people just walked away, evidently unmoved. However, God worked in the hearts of some of those attending that session. The words of Paul stuck in their minds and hearts; they believed! Don't give up because you don't immediately see positive results from your efforts. God knows the hearts of people and He has a plan!

Galatians 6:4 says, *"Each one should test his own actions. Then he can take pride in himself, without comparing himself to anybody else, for each one should carry his own load."*

Shop Prayers

I have a woodworking shop in the back yard. I'll brag for just a moment. I know, Christians aren't supposed to brag are they? Forgive me, but there are just a few things I want you to know related to the shop. It is a two story building. When I built it, I added central air, feeling that would be about as cheap as taking wall space for window-type air conditioners and floor space for a heater. It contains a bathroom with the sink on the shop side of the wall. Hey, if I misbehaved and had to go to the dog house, I had a good place to go.

Among the items I have made are a table-top speaker's lectern for a Sunday school class, computer desk, roll-top desk, English style utility stand, etc. I have never sold an item, but have given them away or employed them in our house or shop.

I often talk to the Lord as I work. You do not always have to stop what you are doing to have a conversation with God. If I make it through a difficult procedure with no problems, I thank God. Sometime I ask for His help in what I'm doing. I remember one time having a difficult process pending but thought I did not have a good tool for it. I asked for the Lord's help, then I opened a cabinet and there was exactly the tool I needed. It had been in the cabinet for the 18 years the shop had been built. I had not needed it before and had forgotten all about it. The Lord is interested in our communication with Him, even in our everyday activities.

I also treasure the private time when I need to offer special thanks, ask for guidance in ministry, ask forgiveness, intercessory prayer for others or simply praise my heavenly Father and Jesus my Savior! You can talk with your Father anytime, not just at "official" times set aside. Those are important too.

In Ephesians 6:18, Paul says, *"And pray in the Spirit on all occasions with all kinds of prayers and requests."* Are you doing this? Now is a good time to start.

Two Fish with One Hook

When our children, Gary and Jeannette, were small, Nora and I took them fishing at a little stream near Fort Worth. We all had a good time together and the children were learning to fish. I had a simple line with a hook and bait on it. After a few minutes I felt a tug and gave the line a little jerk to set the hook. When I pulled the line in we were all surprised. Not just one fish but two were on the line. Impossible? I would have thought so too. One fish had taken the hook. Another fish had latched onto a little wad of something the line had picked up and did not let go. It was about six inches above the hooked fish. I wasn't able to convince them that it was just my fishing skill.

Do you ever have the "impossible" happen? How do you explain it? Do you try to attribute it to some special plan or action of yours?

When unusually good things happen, it's easy to take credit. Or, you might say, "I was just lucky." Really? Could it be that God had a hand in it? God either causes or allows things to take place. Instead of "good luck" I prefer the phrase, "good fortune" or "blessed." God will allow or cause good fortune to come our way. We are blessed. He may allow or cause bad fortune to happen to us when we deserve it, or to teach us something. There is no such thing as luck. Let's get rid of that word.

Job recognized that God is in charge. When his wife told him to curse God and die, he replied, *"Shall we accept good from God and not trouble?"* (Job 2:10). 1 Peter 4:19 says, *"So then, those who suffer according to God's will should commit themselves to their faithful*

Creator and continue to do good." Also, in Lamentations 3:32 we find these words, *"Though He brings grief, He will show compassion, so great is His unfailing love."* God may give or refuse permission.

After the relationship between Jacob and his father-in-law Laban, for whom Jacob worked, had deteriorated and Jacob was planning to take his family and possessions and escape back to Canaan, Jacob said, *"…God has not allowed him to harm me"* (Genesis 31:7). Jacob could have said, "I've been lucky." Instead he recognized that God was in charge.

Get rid of the terms, "luck" and "lucky!"

Fish from Another Leader

One time my family was fishing from the bank at Lake Arlington in Texas. We had not caught much, but one catch was unusual. I felt the tug on my line, but as I drew it in there was no fish on the hook. My hook had caught a leader that had broken loose from someone else's line with a fish on it. There were no other people fishing close to us, so I could not have crossed anyone else's line. How fortunate! I was blessed by another person's effort.

That's the way it is in life. You will often benefit from another's efforts without the person even knowing that he or she had impacted your life. Sometimes you don't even know, or remember, who implanted an idea in your mind or started a project, left unfinished for you to finish. But God does, and he allowed you to pick up on it. God has a purpose in such an action. It will fit into His plan for your life.

When some in the church at Corinth were divided over which minister they followed, Paul reminded them that the ministry to them was a combined effort. He said, *"I planted the seed, Apollos watered it, but God made it grow"* (1 Corinthians 3:6). In chapter 9 Paul speaks to the matter of shared efforts. After posing the question of who serves as a soldier at his own expense, and stating that in the law of Moses it is written, *"Don't muzzle an ox while it is treading out the grain"* (implying that it is a joint effort between the ox and the one feeding it), he says in verse 10, *"Surely He says this for us doesn't He? Yes, this was written for us, because when the plowman plows and the thresher threshes, they ought to do so in the hope of sharing in the harvest."* Perhaps you and someone else have complementary skills. Is there a way you can join efforts to assist in the ministry of the church or community?

Roping Fish

One more fish story. Each one of these is true. I have worked on a ranch as a teenager, but had never thought of roping fish until one day I realized it really could be done. We were living at Hatch New Mexico during some of my early high school years. The Rio Grande River was nearby and the water was clear enough.

In the summer I was working in an electric motor shop rewinding motors. We had several sizes of copper wire on spools to meet the needs of various types and sizes of motors. I remembered that from the bridge across the river, I could look down and see the fish. An idea hit me. I could take size #15 wire, make a loop on one end, like we used to do with a lariat rope and rope some of those fish. My boss let me have enough wire for a friend and myself that would reach from the bridge to the water.

I found that I could guide the loop over the fish's head to just behind the gills; then I would yank the wire to close the loop around the fish and draw it up to the bridge. Even when the wire would rub against the fish while trying to rope it, the fish would only wiggle a little and not run from it. Well, in our part of the country, we'll rope about anything we can.

Have you ever been asked to participate or lead in a ministry of the church, but you thought, "I could never do that?" Or, as a pastor, has an idea for an unusual ministry occurred to you and the though kept coming to your mind, "That would be impossible, especially for this church?" Were you convinced the idea was from the Lord? Then it is possible and you can do what He is presenting to you! Perhaps the Lord is encouraging you to exercise your faith and depend more on Him! Go to it!

Isaiah told Ahaz, when Judah was threatened by an overwhelming enemy, *"If you do not stand firm in your faith, you will not stand at all."* (Isaiah 7:9). We have the same God as Ahaz had, and He is the same yesterday, today and tomorrow. Jesus said, *"...I tell you the truth, if you have faith as small as a mustard seed, you can say to this mountain, 'Move from here to there,' and it will move. Nothing will be impossible for you"* What about the mountains in your life, those that seem impossible to hurdle? Go rope some fish!

Wonderfully Blessed

Sometimes we need to pause and consider all the ways God has blessed us, even when we were not always blessing Him. We need to thank Him for His Fatherly care, His precious Son and the eternal life He has given us. When I look back over my life, I see the times the Lord has used caring discipline to draw me back into a close walk with Him. I may not have liked the discipline at the time, but later could see it was an act of love from my heavenly Father.

God gave me caring Christ-loving parents, brothers and sisters. He provided me with a beautiful, caring and faithful wife. The Lord gave us wonderful children who grew to love Him and married outstanding Christian spouses. Both of our grandchildren also are believers and married caring spouses. God is good!

I have been richly blessed in ministry, with preaching opportunities even while in high school, and pastorates throughout my college and seminary years. In the early 1960s I left the pastoral ministry for a while with the excuse, "God can use men in business," which He can if that's where God wants him. That's not where He wanted me, but after bringing me back to where He wanted me, He used the skills I acquired for His glory.

Besides my earlier pastorates in New Mexico, God allowed me the opportunity of being the pastor of a wonderful church in Dallas, Texas and then in Maryland. After six years as a pastor at Kingsville, Maryland the Lord called me to direct two Baptist associations in that state. Nora and I were both commissioned as home missionaries (now called North American missionaries). We served as missionaries during my entire twenty years as director of missions. Nora retired from teaching school to become my administrative assistant.

God has given me the privilege of preaching in at least sixteen states and has allowed me to be a conference leader at Ridgecrest in North Carolina which is the Southern Baptist conference center. Since moving to Texas I have had the privilege of preaching the message for the state WMU (Woman's Missionary Union) annual conference, among other works. The preaching opportunities in the various states consisted of pastorates, individual preaching engagements, revival meetings and world mission conferences which were arranged by the Home Mission Board (now named North American Mission Board). The number of home, foreign and special missionaries for a world missions conference would equal the number of churches enrolled. In the eight days of a conference (Sunday through Sunday), each of us would speak in ten churches. These churches would all be members of one association.

If we will be open to the Lord's direction, He will show us where and how He wants us to serve. There are plenty of opportunities for you to share the gospel of the Lord Jesus Christ and be involved in the ministry of discipleship. Just ask the Lord for direction and join Him in His work; He will open doors for you.

Jesus said, *"As long as it is day, we must do the work of Him who sent me. Night is coming, when no one can work"* (John 9:4). Just ask God for His leadership. In Matthew 21:22 Jesus said, *"If you believe, you will receive whatever you ask for in prayer."* He is talking about believers whose will is in line with God's will.

When someone was needed to replace the vacancy left by Judas as one of the apostles, they prayed and Lord led them to Matthias (Acts 1:21-26). James says in his letter, chapter 5, verses17-18, *"Elijah was a man just like us. He prayed earnestly that it would not rain, and it did not rain on the land for three and a half years. Again he prayed and the heavens gave rain, and the earth produced its crops."* God will hear your prayers too, if you are truly seeking His will. Ask Him and He will open the future for you.

Inspiration from Chief Deerfoot

Chief Joe Deerfoot was an Apache Indian who headed the Navajo tour in Northwest New Mexico. Seem strange? The website, Indians. org tells us "It is believed that because their language is similar, that the Apache and Navajo were once a lone ethnic group." According to huddlestonfamily.org he would lead "Gallup's Inter-Tribal Indian Ceremonial parade riding his paint stallion Bobby. The horse was trained to perform tricks and would bow and rear for the crowds." Chief Deerfoot and his wife, Ora, were active members of First Baptist Church in Gallup, New Mexico. I understand he died in 1966 at 77 years old.

I first saw Chief Deerfoot in an all-school assembly when I was in the second grade in Melrose, New Mexico. Later, when I was a sophomore in high school in Hatch, New Mexico, he appeared in an all-school assembly there.

Chief Deerfoot shared about the Navajo culture and a little about the Apache. He showed us examples of pottery, weavings, and stone and bead work of the Navaho tribe and related characteristic of some other tribes. He also set up a target with a large rotating wheel supporting two or three balloons. He then went to the opposite end of the stage holding a bow and arrow. He stood with his back to the rotating wheel, then quickly turned around and shot the arrow hitting a balloon. He repeated this after taking another arrow from the quiver on his back.

My Dad was pastor of First Baptist Church in Hatch and had invited Chief Deerfoot to have lunch with us. He was a Christian and his visit at the table and following was an inspiration to us. Some years later Dad was the missionary for a Baptist association of churches in Southwest Colorado and Northwest New Mexico. This included Gallup where Chief Deerfoot lived. He and Dad became good friends, and Chief Deerfoot made a beautiful watchband of turquoise stones and gave it to Dad.

We can learn a lot from other cultures and can benefit by shared relationships. Today, a few of our churches remain isolated from other races and cultures. A church can be so self-focused hat it fails to grow and tends to gradually diminish. We need to open up. Share and make friends across cultures. This will help us all to grow and understand that the race or culture does not make one group any better than another.

I know of Christian missionaries who are Indian, Black, Hispanic, and Asian. Most work across cultures. After all, the races and cultures are simply a part of God's artistic creation! Jesus healed the son of a Roman centurion, converted a Samarian woman and commanded us to go into all the world with the Good News.

In John 8:12 Jesus said, *"I am the light of the world,"* But in Matthew 5:14 He said, *"You are the light of the world."* He followed this in verse 16 with *"… let your light shine before men that they may see your good deeds and praise your Father in heaven."* In comparison with the bulb and reflector headlights automobiles used to have, we are reflectors of Christ's light and therefore are a part of that light. If the bulb had no reflector, it would be practically ineffective. He did not say you are the light for a particular group or type. In John 3:16 he said, *"For God so loved the world…"* Do you have any friends of other races or cultures? Go out and cultivate some of those friendships; break down the barriers. You'll be happy you did! They can be a blessing to you and you can bless them.

Ridgecrest Leaders, the Snow Won

A conference leaders meeting was scheduled at Ridgecrest Baptist Assembly in preparation for Home Missions Week there. I was to catch a plane in Baltimore and after arriving at Ashville would rent a car for two others from D.C. and me to go the short distance to Ridgecrest.

A huge winter snow storm moved in and the Baltimore plane would be delayed for two hours, so I drove on to the D.C. airport to catch a connecting plane scheduled to leave with a shorter delay. Boarding with me there were the other two conference leaders from the area. The trip to Ashville was uneventful. I rented the car and we went to the conference center.

We waited for the meeting leader from the Home Mission Board in Atlanta, Georgia. After some time, I received a call that the Atlanta Airport was closed because of the storm and we would skip the leaders meeting. Instead, we would get together briefly after arriving for Home Missions Week. Can you believe it? We were able to fly from D.C. which got a worse dose of the storm, but the Atlanta airport, much further south, was closed! Well, further north the cities and counties had the equipment to deal with the snow. Southern states are not likely to be that equipped.

All we could do was drive back to Ashville, turn in the car and fly back to D.C. It's not often that I have been able to take a leisurely plane trip to another state and return in the same day! Actually, we would have preferred to have had the meeting.

Things don't always work out as planned and you have to move to plan B, or perhaps move in a completely new direction. That happened to the apostle Paul. He and his companions had planned to preach the gospel in the province of Asia. When God prevented it, he didn't give up and say, "Well, I tried." Acts16:6 tells us, *"Paul and his companions traveled throughout the region of Phrygia and Galatia, having been kept by the Holy Spirit from preaching the word in the province of Asia."* Then they wanted to enter Bithynia but God wouldn't let them. Verses 8 through 10 say, *"So they passed by Mysia and went down to Troas. During the night Paul had a vision of a man in Macedonia standing and begging him, 'Come over into Macedonia and help us.' After Paul had seen the vision, we got ready at once to leave for Macedonia, concluding that God had called us to preach the gospel to them."*

If your plans don't work out, it may be that God has other plans for you. Don't give up. Ask God to show you where He wants you to go, or what He wants you to do. It may be to just look where God is at work and join Him!

Indian Paintings with a Rattlesnake

When I was pastor of First Baptist Church in Santa Rosa, New Mexico, I also led the Royal Ambassador group for boys. This included guidance for living and learning about world missions, we also had craft activities.

One day I decided to take the boys on a hike. The church was at the edge of town and out from there was open unimproved land. We hiked for close to a mile and came upon a wide crevice in the ground. It was about ten feet wide, ten feet deep and probably fifty to sixty feet long. We noticed what appeared to be some painting on the wall, so we decided to investigate.

We climbed down into the crevice and noticed ancient Indian paintings on both walls. As we worked our way to the far end, suddenly we heard a familiar, tdtdtdtdtd, the warning from a rattlesnake. As we glanced toward the direction of the sound, we saw a den of rattlers. We decided we had seen enough and began to work our way out, hoping the way was clear.

Hey, this was an experience to remember and the Lord protected us. These were a type of snakes that give warnings. Not all snakes do that. I think the Lord likes for us to look over His creation and admire it, all aspects of it. Give Him the Glory for His mighty power and wisdom and artistic ability!

I enjoy listening to the lightning, thunder and rain. The lightning and thunder remind me of God's mighty power and the rain demonstrates His provision. There is no reason to worry about lightning strikes, just take caution. Worry doesn't change anything but the worrier, so you might as well relax and enjoy it. Proverbs 3:19 tells us why the earth is so magnificent, *"By wisdom the Lord laid the earth's foundations, by understanding He set the heavens in place; by His knowledge the deeps were divided, and the clouds let drop the dew."*

Stopped at the Wall

On a trip to Israel with a group one of our stops on a Sabbath day was at the Western Wall of Jerusalem. It is often called the Wailing Wall because men often line up at the base of it to say their prayers, which many interpret as a wailing sound.

As we stood a short distance from the wall our group leader read a passage of scripture and shared a brief devotional. We then were told about the history of the wall and about the actions we were observing. A lady in the group was taking notes. A security agent noticed her note taking and came over to the group. He said, "You cannot take notes on the Sabbath." He stopped her and had her put her notepad away.

Note taking was considered working. However, it was ok for the bus driver to transport us to the site. I had a small recorder in my shirt pocket recording everything that was said. I wonder if that violated the Sabbath rules. Before the trip, our material warned travelers who rent a car not to drive into certain cities on the Sabbath because the car would be stoned.

I cannot help but admire the dedication of many Israelites to their beliefs, although I cannot agree with their theology. They are a beautiful people and the Messiah, our Savior, was repeatedly prophesied in their Scripture, which is also a part of our Christian Bible. I wish they understood the Object of those prophesies and His fulfillment of the Law, as well as His gift of eternal life through faith.

What about you? Are you still struggling, trying to earn your way to heaven? You will never make it that way. Ephesians 2:8-9 makes it plain. Paul, speaking to believers, but also for the benefit of unbelievers, said, *"For it is by grace you have been saved, through faith – and this not from yourselves, it is the gift of God – not by works, so that no one can boast."*

You cannot earn salvation, no matter how "good" you are. God wants to <u>give</u> you a full and meaningful life on this earth and then take you to live with Him for all eternity. He even sacrificed His own Son to pay for your sins. Jesus, the Father's Son, also loves you so much He was willing to go to the cross, taking your sins on Him. He was buried and on the third day was raised back to life. But you can only benefit from this if you are willing to receive the gift He offers. You receive the gift by placing your faith in Jesus Christ and letting Him direct your life.

After Jesus rose from the grave, He spent 40 days instructing His disciples. In fact, He was seen by over 500 people on one occasion. After the 40 days He ascended into heaven as people watched. Romans 6:23 says, *"For the wages of sin is death, but the gift of God is eternal life in Christ Jesus our Lord."* If you do not know the Lord, the issue is now in your lap. You will make a decision now – either to accept His offer or to refuse it. Either way that is a decision, and it has eternal consequence.

Europe: What a Tour!

When Ron, our son-in-law, was in the military service and stationed in Germany, Nora and I went to visit him, our daughter Jeannette, and our grandchildren, Joshua and Jessica. While there they took us on a tour of portions of Germany, Switzerland, Lichtenstein, Netherlands, and Austria. Outstanding memories linger relating to each of these places.

In the storybook village of Oberammergau, about 45 miles from Munich, a world famous Passion Play has been performed every ten years since 1634, currently from May through September. Over 1500 adults and 500 children are normally involved in the production; all are residents of that small village. We visited the location from which this production is performed and were given a fantastic tour backstage.

On this German tour I was struck with some of the construction practices in Germany. Residences often had narrow stairways, through which it would be difficult or impossible to take large furniture such as a piano or large dresser. However they had a solution for this. From a large double-paneled second story window would be an extended arm with a built-in track and pulley. Straps or ropes would be attached to the furniture piece on the ground and raised to the extended arm, and then easily pulled in to the house. These extended arms on houses were a common site.

Grass roofs on houses were quite common in the Bavarian region. I thought they were just on houses of people who could not afford regular tile or shingle roofs, but the tour guide said these were the most expensive types. It seems that the grass was of a type that stays short and needs little maintenance. Some houses had only a portion of the roof covered this way. I was told that this is usually when the owner cannot afford doing the whole roof at one time. I am told that thermal advantages of these green roofs include better heat retention during the winter and reflecting and absorbing solar radiation during the summer months. The sod is laid over a coat of waterproofing.

In Amsterdam we were impressed with the extensive fields with various kinds and colors of tulips. In fact, we ordered a select group of the bulbs to be sent us in the U.S. They really brightened our flower bed.

Another ingenious thing we noticed was the way hay was stored. I think this could be attractive to small hay growers in the United States. It consisted of three or four very tall posts that could hold up a four sided roof with holes for each post. With the attached ropes and pulleys, the roof could be raised or lowered to keep it always close to the top of the hay for rain and wind protection.

In Switzerland we toured a historic church. We were amazed at the extremely tall and steep mountains of that country, and we stayed at an inn in a village just below some of these.

The innkeepers owned a herd of deer. They were domesticated just like cattle are here in the United States. My grandchildren, Joshua and Jessica, and I walked along the side of the deer pasture. Some deer came over to the fence and nibbled grass from our hands.

Liechtenstein is one of the smallest nations in the world. Instead of its own currency this constitutional monarchy uses the Swiss franc. The official language is German, generally spoken with an Alemannic dialect of German. I have learned that religious education, either Roman Catholicism or Protestantism, is required in the schools. Catholicism is the national religion according to the constitution. We enjoyed the beauty of its rugged mountains and the country in general.

We also went to Innsbruck, Austria. At least two winter Olympics have been held there. The highlight of that stop for me was being able to go to the top of the ski jump used in the Olympics and look down at the view. I could hardly believe my eyes. From that great height the skier would gain speed and make the jump. Then, while soaring through the air, the view included a cemetery straight ahead across the road. Of course the landing and crowd would be before that, but I wondered about what might invade the skier's mind.

On the way home from Germany, we changed planes in Paris. We could view the city but did not leave the airport. Actually the greatest thing about the trip was the time we were able to enjoy with family stationed so far from home. This was a trip to remember!

All of the views we experienced impressed upon us the magnificence of God's creation. Just imagine the power, wisdom, artistic ability and universal existence required to put it all together! We have a great God! It's good to explore what He has made.

God says in Isaiah 45:12, *"It is I who made the earth and created mankind upon it. My own hands stretched out the heavens; I marshaled the starry hosts."* The Psalmist says in Psalm 139:13, *"You created my inmost being, you knit me together in my mother's womb. I praise you because I am fearfully and wonderfully made; your works are wonderful. I know that full well."*

Do you take time to explore God's universe and stand amazed at its magnificence. And remember, He created mankind in His image. He wants your submission to His direction of your life. He loves you so much He wants to have you with Him for all eternity.

Fun With German War Prisoners

In 1947 I was a sophomore in high school and living in Hatch, a small town in New Mexico. World War II began in 1939 and ended in 1945, but a German Prisoner of War Camp was still located in Hatch. It was about a block or two from our house. With the wire mesh fences we were able to see the prisoners move freely about and would have been able to converse with them if we could understand German.

One day a snow storm hit Hatch and I had an idea. I shared it with a friend. We went over to the camp, made us some snowballs. As one of the men was exiting the mess hall, we pounded him and a few of the balls went into the mess hall.

This got the action going. Some of the prisoners started making snowballs and returning the fire. Of course they outnumbered us. So when the next snowstorm came there were more of us. The prisoners could tell that this was all for fun and not out of anger or hatred. We had a good time with them and they probably had not had so much fun since their capture.

These German men had been forced into Hitler's army to fight Americans or any others according to location. It did not mean that they agreed with Hitler's hatred of the Jews or his ambition to rule the world. They were not bad men just because they had been military enemies.

God loved the German prisoners just as He loves us. In fact, many of them may have been Christians.

In Luke 6:27 Jesus said, *"But I tell you who hear me: Love your enemies, do good to those who hate you, bless those who curse you, pray for those who mistreat you."* Romans 12:18 and 19 tells us to live at peace with everyone and not take revenge. Where there are problems, leave it in God's hands.

How do you handle your relationships with those who are different from you – in attitude, actions, race, culture, aggressiveness or other ways? Do you let small differences annoy you and impact your relationships? OR, Do you turn these things over to God and trust Him with them?

Right now may be the time you need to talk to God about it.

The Post Skull
Practice Question

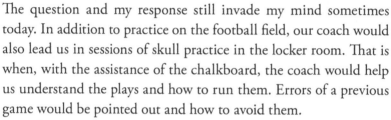

The question and my response still invade my mind sometimes today. In addition to practice on the football field, our coach would also lead us in sessions of skull practice in the locker room. That is when, with the assistance of the chalkboard, the coach would help us understand the plays and how to run them. Errors of a previous game would be pointed out and how to avoid them.

After one of our skull sessions, before going out to the field for practice, Larry, one of the players, called me aside and surprised me with a question. He asked, "How can I be saved?" My answer was, "Just put your trust in the Lord." Then I went on out to practice with the rest of the team. He had asked the most important of questions and I had brushed it off with a short answer. I made no attempt to get with him at another time to talk about it.

Years later, after we had moved away, that event kept coming back to me. On one occasion I tried to locate Larry, but he had moved and I was unable to find him. That still comes to mind sometimes. Perhaps the Lord is using it to prompt me never to let such an opportunity pass again. I know I still walk passed some doors for witness the Lord opens for me.

How about you? We both have room for improvement. Let's agree to put forth the effort to stay aware of the Lord's leadership through a study of His printed word, personal communication with

Him and listening to the Holy Spirit who helps us understand God's printed word and His answers to our prayers.

A passage that addresses all of this is found in Ephesians 6:14-18, where Paul tells us to put on the full armor of God, *"Stand firm then, with the belt of truth buckled around your waist, with the breastplate of righteousness in place, and with your feet fitted with readiness that comes from the gospel of peace. In addition to all of this, take up the shield of faith, with which you can extinguish all the flaming arrows of the evil one. Take the helmet of salvation and the sword of the Spirit, which is the word of God. And pray in the Spirit on all occasions with all kinds of prayers and requests. With this in mind be alert ..."*

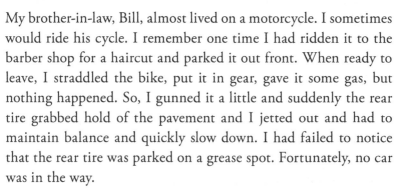

Motorcycle Hit the Dirt

My brother-in-law, Bill, almost lived on a motorcycle. I sometimes would ride his cycle. I remember one time I had ridden it to the barber shop for a haircut and parked it out front. When ready to leave, I straddled the bike, put it in gear, gave it some gas, but nothing happened. So, I gunned it a little and suddenly the rear tire grabbed hold of the pavement and I jetted out and had to maintain balance and quickly slow down. I had failed to notice that the rear tire was parked on a grease spot. Fortunately, no car was in the way.

Bill would always remove the windshield on his motorcycles. He evidently liked the wind in his face. I used to sometimes hop on it early in the morning just after getting out on bed and blast out a short distance on the highway and return. The cold wind in my face made sure I was wide awake.

But the time I remember most was after Bill had set the carburetor speed jets. He wanted to check it out and invited me to go with him. I sat behind him. At Hatch, New Mexico an irrigation canal with a dirt road along the side of it was near our house. We used to swim in the canal. Well, we were on the canal dirt road sailing along at a rather high speed and suddenly met the ditch-rider, who maintains the canal, in his car. The road was only wide enough for one car, so bill laid the cycle down into the dirt canal bank. He ended up over the handlebars and I was on the gas tank. The leg-protection bar did its work, digging in so that our legs just touched the surface, but the foot-rest was bent back. Neither of us was injured and Bill straightened out the foot-rest after arriving home. I could only thank the Lord for His protective care.

At that point in Bill's life he was sort of a dare-devil. He later was converted and became an active Christian and caring husband for my sister, Wilma.

Sometimes we lose our alertness and fail to take precaution. We may also miss the opportunities around us. We get into trouble. When the Lord protects us from our own mistakes, do we remember to thank Him and learn from the lesson? God may also allow us to suffer for our mistakes when we ignore His cautions in order to help us know that we are not self-dependant and need to rely more fully on Him.

The psalmist said, *"It was good for me to be afflicted so that I might learn from your decrees"* (Psalm 119:71). But the psalmist also prayed in 5:11, *"But let all who take refuge in you be glad; let them ever sing for joy. Spread your protection over them, that those who love your name may rejoice in you."* Paul tells us in Colossians 3:17, *"And whatever you do, whether in word or deed, do it all in the name of the Lord Jesus, giving thanks to God the Father, through Him."* There's you order. Get with it.

B.B. McKinney Experience

What a privilege! When I was a student at Eastern New Mexico University, the Baptist Student Center invited B.B. McKinney for an evangelistic emphasis, primarily conducted in the Baptist Student Center adjoining the campus. I believe this took place in the fall of 1950. B.B. died two years later. I was selected to give Mr. McKinney a tour of the campus.

For those who may not know who Baylus Benjamin McKinney was, I'll give a brief background. He lived from July 1886 until September 1952 and was known by his initials. In addition to other ministries B.B. was a prolific Hymn writer. According to several sources, including the Southern Baptist Historical Library and Archives, he wrote both the words and music for 149 gospel hymns and songs and composed the music for 114 texts by other authors. He was editor of the Broadman Hymnal and many of his hymns appear in the Baptist Hymnal that later replaced the Broadman. His works appear in many other Hymnals as well.

While B.B. was with us at ENMU he wrote a chorus and we sang it at least once before the week was over. I do not remember the name or words. Then on the final night he was with us, which was on Sunday, we met at Calvary Baptist Church in Portales. Mr. McKinney announced that if someone would stand up and sing the course he had written, he would give his manuscript to that person. Immediately a music student stood up and sang it. He received the manuscript.

Mr. McKinney related well to the students, although there

was quite an age difference. He was a committed Christian who lived what he preached. He has made tremendous contributions to Christian music, and therefore to our worship services.

Have you thought about leaving a continued witness after your time on earth is completed? Your impact on your children and grandchildren will carry on for generations. Make it worthwhile. Also you may leave a work from which others will benefit, to the glory of God. Perhaps by using a gift or talent God has given you, there is something else you can leave, whether written, established, artistically produced or constructed. For instance, I hope and pray that this book relating experiences of my lifetime will have an impact on someone's life.

Words mean little if not complimented by example. Have you heard the expression, "Deeds speak louder than words"? There's a lot of truth to that. After Jesus had washed his disciples' feet, which may have been dirty after walking dusty trails in sandals, he said, *"I have set you an example that you should do as I have done for you"* (John 13:15). After the apostle Paul had said that he did not seek his *"own good but the good of many, so they may be saved,"* he said in 1 Corinthians 11:1, *"Follow my example, as I follow the example of Christ."*

Our words must be supported by action!

Head-Hunters, Now Believers

I wish to share with you some of my experiences in working with members of the Chin tribe of Myanmar (Burma). There are several tribes among the Chin people in what used to be Burma. They are located in a rugged mountainous region in the southern part of Northwest Myanmar. Collectively, they are often referred to as the Chin tribe, now organized into the Chin state. The people with whom I worked were of a tribe which, at one time, had been a tribe of notorious head-hunters.

A tribe member told me that a Baptist missionary, Adoniram Judson, walked a great distance to their tribe risking his life to bring them the gospel. This was in the 1800s. Today there is a strong Baptist convention in the Chin state consisting of 28 Associations and I am told that 90% of the Chin population are Christian, even though most of Myanmar is Buddhist.

Often when people come to the United States from the Chin tribe, as well as from some other places in the world, they will take on meaningful new American names. Christians often take on biblical names. That is true with the persons I wish to share with you.

When I was director of missions for Blue Ridge and Central Baptist Associations in Maryland, a member of one of the churches told me of a man in jail who had accepted Christ as his Savior. I visited the man and found that he had married a woman from a tribe in Myanmar. After he was out of jail I visited the couple and was informed that other tribal members had immigrated to the area and were wondering how to begin a church here, as well as getting a place to meet. The pastor would be Moses. I arranged for Sunday use of space in one of the public schools. As the group grew, Peter, a Chin evangelist, arrived and became a part of the group. He and Moses were the primary leaders.

After South End Baptist Church in Frederick, Maryland completed the building of a new sanctuary, the church made the old sanctuary available to the new Chin church. The congregation rapidly grew as there were other Chin people in the D. C. and Maryland area.

According to a Chin member, the Myanmar government only allowed Christian messages and music on the radio for a short time before Christmas.

One day the Foreign Mission Board, now the International Mission Board, informed me that the director of their work for Southeast Asia would soon be on his way to Myanmar for Judson Day and would arrange for a delayed plane connection at the Newark, New Jersey airport if we would like to meet with him. Because of the great contribution Adoniram Judson made to Burma as a translator during the Anglo-Burmese War (no one else spoke both Burmese and English), there has been an annual Adoniram Judson Celebration Day ever since. Actually Judson had been in jail for some time because of his Christian beliefs, but he was released because an interpreter was needed.

I took Moses and Peter to the meeting at the airport. There was a good exchange of information that could be helpful on the trip.

Peter was one of the newest arrivals from the Chin. The automatic doors which opened when approached continued to catch him by surprise. We stopped at McDonalds on the way back. Going to the restroom, he had more surprises. When the commode automatically flushed he jumped and could not understand how it knew when an how to do that. He walked over to the washbasin, and while trying to see how to turn the water on he happened to run his hand under the faucet. The water immediately started. It was another mystery to him. There was more. When he went to the hand drier and his hands happened under it, the drier immediately started. All of this was a mystery. Peter could not imagine how these devices knew when to do their work. Among the Chin, and perhaps in Burma itself, this technology was unknown. I think this was an interesting trip for us all.

The Chin Christians are a wonderful people. They are respectful, and the ones I met were active in sharing the gospel with others, especially the Chin since they spoke the same language.

No matter what language, nationality, race or ethnic group, as Christians we are all in the same family as brothers and sisters. We are in God's family. We are blood kin, through the blood of Jesus Christ shed on the cross of Calvary.

How do you relate to people of other races or ethnic groups? Remember that God loves us all and tells us that our mission is to be for the whole world. Can you swallow prior feelings toward people of another race and let God's love flow through you to them? You have brothers and sisters among them also.

Jesus said in Mathew 7:1-2, *"Do not judge, or you too will be judged. For in the same way you judge others, you will be judged, and with the same measure you use, it will be measured to you."* In verse 12 He says, *"So in everything, do to others what you would have them do to you..."* When Phillip, who was not Black, met the Ethiopian who was Black, he did not hesitate to share the gospel with him. He sat by him on the chariot and rode along with him. When the Ethiopian accepted Christ as Savior, Phillip baptized him. He followed the direction of the Holy Spirit. There is no evidence of any reluctance. The record of this is found in Acts 8:26-40.

Even though Jesus was born and raised as a Jew, He traveled through Samaria and saved a Samarian woman and others of that population. Samarians were hated by the Jews. Jesus healed a Roman centurion's servant and gave an extraordinary compliment about the centurion's faith.

In Matthew 28:18-20, before his ascension to heaven, Jesus instructed us to make disciples of all nations. God loves all people and we should too.

How extensive is your love? Room for improvement?

World Series
Signed Baseball

In the spring of 1970, during baseball season, there was a community auction. One item was a baseball that had been signed by all of the Baltimore Orioles team. Later that season the Orioles won the World Series. I was able to buy the ball for five dollars and gave it to our son, Gary. After some time, Gary looked for the ball but could not find it. It seemed to have been lost. Forty-seven years later, following my wife Nora's death, we were going through mountains of possessions in view of yard sales and gifts to charity organizations. What do you know!? That World Series ball with all of the Orioles' signatures surfaced!

Our daughter, Jeannette bought a display container for it and I drew up documentation to include in the display. At the time of this writing, Gary was greatly surprised when he learned that the ball had been found, and I handed it to him.

Have you had any great surprises lately? The Bible speaks of a coming great surprise for many. In his letter to the Thessalonian church, the apostle Paul wrote in 1 Thessalonians 5:1-6, *"Now, brothers, about times and dates we do not need to write to you, for you know very well that the day of the Lord will come like a thief in the night. While people are saying, 'Peace and safety,' destruction will come on them suddenly, as labor pains on a pregnant woman, and they will not escape.*

"But you, brothers are not in darkness so that the day should surprise

you like a thief. You are all sons of the light and sons of the day. We do not belong to the night or to the darkness. So then, let us not be like the others who are asleep, but let us be alert and self-controlled."

Are you prepared for that day? A surprise may come before that time. Death can strike you at any moment, by body malfunction or accident. Your destiny must be determined before that. No matter how your life has been, God loves you so much that He wants you to be with Him for all eternity. His love for you is so great that He sacrificed His own Son to take you sins on him and erase your slate clean. Jesus carried your sins to the grave. After three days the Father brought Him back to life. He appeared on earth for 40 days instructing his disciples and then ascended to heaven. Over 500 people saw him alive at one time after His resurrection from the grave.

You cannot be good enough to earn the full and meaningful life on this earth and eternal life in heaven. It is God's gift to you, but it is not yours until you accept it. What you need to do is talk to God. Repent of your sins and ask Jesus to save you and become the Lord of your life. After that, you are to seek to live a life that will please Him.

A two-way conversation should follow regularly in your life. God primarily speaks to you through His printed word, the Bible. Read it daily. You primarily speak to God through prayer. God's Holy Spirit will help you to understand God's printed word and to understand God's answers to your prayers, as well as how to apply it all to your life.

If you are one seeking salvation, the Gospel of John is a good place to start your reading. Also, Romans 3:23 tells us, *"For all have sinned and fall short of the glory of God,"* and 6:23 says, *"For the wages of sin is death, but the gift of God is eternal life in Christ Jesus our Lord."* Ephesians 2:8-9 states how this gift is received. There Paul writes to church members at Ephesus, *"For it is by grace you have been saved, through faith – and this not from yourselves, it is the gift of God – not by works so that no one can boast."* Find an evangelical church, such as Baptist for instance, and make your decision public. Then enjoy the fellowship and study and grow with the congregation.

The Egyptian Experience

The trip had been an exciting one, flying on Jordanian airlines from Baltimore to Jordan and transported to Jerusalem by bus. After time in Israel, Nora and I, along with others in the group, headed for Egypt. In the clearance process we were individually searched, x-rayed and required to point our cameras toward the ceiling of the search booth and click them to show that they were not weapons. Then one of the group's luggage was held so the group leader would have to make a private payment to the inspector. After that we were cleared to go.

We boarded the bus headed for Egypt. Crossing the Sinai desert, we saw many of the remains of armored vehicles destroyed during the eight days war. Arab nomads living in some of them had added tent-like additions.

Every few miles the road would make a 90⁰ turn. At each turn was a checkpoint with soldiers. We were not checked there, they would generally change the guard on the bus. The soldier on the bus was there for the protection of us Americans.

As we were riding along, the soldier suddenly looked straight at Nora and pointed his finger at her. Nora was startled and scared. Actually, he was pointing his finger at her necklace. We had bought the necklace in Israel. It had her name in three languages, Hebrew, Arabic and English. The guard had noticed the Arabic spelling and said, "My wife Nora." There was no threat at all, just a moment of excitement. Having some conversation with him was a good thing.

In Cairo, it seemed that there were soldiers on every block. They were often squatted down or sitting on the sidewalk with their backs against the wall of the building. Their guns were visibly with them.

To go through a Muslim museum we had to take our shoes off and the women were to have something on their head, even if it was a sheet of paper held by bobby pins. We also had an exciting time in the Great Pyramid. But I have written elsewhere about the scary event in the pyramid and how this led to a private extended tour of the historic museum in Memphis, so I will not duplicate it here.

All of the above is sort of a reflection of the Christian life. Our life in Christ is exciting, sometimes a little scary. We are encouraged to work with different cultures of people, who often do not believe as we do. Sometimes, for many, it involves a degree of danger, but God is with us and will see us through. We do not need to fear death because God has something better for us. He qualified us through His Son, Jesus Christ.

The trip was a learning experience. It helped cause the Bible to really come alive. The places mentioned can be visualized and the actions imaged in my mind. As Christians, we are to continually be in the process of learning and growing. We have been given God's printed word and must study it regularly. We also learn and grow by being with other Christians in group Bible study, prayer, worship and hearing His word preached.

What about you? Are you really studying God's Word and taking advantage of opportunities to increase your effectiveness in sharing it? Paul tells us in 2 Timothy 2:15, "Do your best to present yourself to God as one approved, a workman who does not need to be ashamed and who correctly handles the word of truth."

As you go about in the world, are you sharing your faith with others by your words and your example? We have a command, not a suggestion, from our Savior in Matthew 28:18-20, *"All authority in heaven and on earth has been given to me. Therefore go and make disciples of all nations, baptizing them in the name of the Father and of the Son and of the Holy Spirit, and teaching them to obey everything I have commanded you. And surely I am with you always, to the very end of the age."* The original language for the word *"go"* gives the meaning of "As you go." However, the rest of that sentence is a command.

We aren't alone when we are fulfilling that command. In Acts 1:8 our savior says, *"But you will receive power when the Holy Spirit comes on you, and you will be my witnesses in Jerusalem, and in all Judea and Samaria, and to the ends of the earth."*

Those locations were used because of where they lived. For us, we might see Jerusalem as our county, Judea as our state, Samaria as our nation, and the rest of the earth is obvious. Wherever we are, we must share the Good News. Have courage! You are not alone. The Holy Spirit is with you and He will help you know what to say and how to say it.

Dad Gave Me the Reins

When we lived on a farm a couple of miles west of Portales, New Mexico, the power for our equipment consisted of two horses. I was in the fourth grade at school. One day Dad was plowing. The walking plow was made of wood. It had a metal, triangular blade to dig the furrows and had two wooden handles for one to hold and guide it. It was pulled by two work horses.

I was walking along behind Dad. After awhile, in about the middle of a row, Dad stopped and motioned for me to come up to the plow. He put my hands on the handles and the reins over my shoulder. Dad let me plow for a way – I said plow, but because of my size I had to reach up for the handles and this probably caused the plow to barely scratch the surface of the ground. But that was O.K. with Dad. He constantly looked for ways to teach me and to show his care.

That's the way it is with our heavenly Father. He has provided His printed word to teach us, and sometimes He uses life experiences to provide lessons. It all shows His love for us.

Are you attending class or playing hooky? Get that Bible out and read it. When life experiences happen that you do not understand, ask God about them. He has provided you with His Holy Spirit who will help you understand His printed word and God's answer to your prayers. Get back in church. There's a lot to learn and experience as you fellowship with brothers and sisters in Christ, study together, listen to the pastor's message and join in worship of the Lord God Almighty.

The apostle Paul tells us in 2nd Timothy 2:15, *"Do your best to present yourself to God as one approved, a workman who does not need to be ashamed and who correctly handles the word of truth."* Hebrews 13:15-16 tells us, *"Through Jesus, therefore, let us continue to offer a sacrifice of praise – the fruit of the lips that confess His name. And do not forget to do good and to share with others, for with such sacrifices God is pleased."* And in 10:25 of Hebrews we are told, *"Let us not give up meeting together, as some are in the habit of doing, but let us encourage one another – and all the more as you see the Day approaching."*

Now you know what the Lord says – so get with it!

Gold Bison Turns Blue

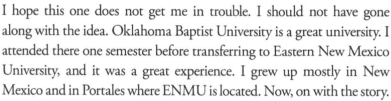

I hope this one does not get me in trouble. I should not have gone along with the idea. Oklahoma Baptist University is a great university. I attended there one semester before transferring to Eastern New Mexico University, and it was a great experience. I grew up mostly in New Mexico and in Portales where ENMU is located. Now, on with the story.

This was in the fall of 1949. We wore a green cap to identify us as freshmen. Each freshman was assigned to an upperclassman for the first semester, sort of an initiation. We were to obey that person unless there was a substantial reason not to.

Professor Bailey had a large house and rented out the upstairs to male students. I rented space there and, wouldn't you know, my assigned upperclassman also was a fellow renter. He had a "bright" idea, "Let's paint the bison blue." He had already bought the paint and brush.

On the oval at the entrance to the campus is the statue of a gold bison. It is on a fairly high pedestal. One night we hid behind some bushes until the night watchman went to a restaurant, about a half mile up the road, for a break. That was our chance. My upperclassman – I have forgotten the term they used – instructed me to climb up to the bison. He then got the paint and brush up to me. Yes, I painted the bison blue. The job was completed and we were on our way before the night watchman returned.

I understand that on a previous year the same thing had happened. Only that time the night watchman was arriving just as the painters were leaving. Another student was walking along the sidewalk, returning from an event. He didn't know what was going on. The paint bucket with the brush was quickly shoved into his hands and the painters fled. The night watchman saw him holding the bucket, stopped him and reported him. He almost got expelled before the administration was convinced he didn't do it.

After the big commotion about the blue bison, my "boss" said, "We are going to paint it gold again." The gold paint and brush were purchased, but we were just a little late. The school had it painted on the day of which night we were going to do the job.

There is more to the story. On homecoming day, my "no green cap guy" had me to climb up to the gold bison with the empty bucket that had dried blue paint on its side, calling for more paint. The campus photographer came running and took a picture. Fortunately, it seems that no one connected the two events. Perhaps the photographer did and kept quiet, because the picture never appeared in the annual. It may be that the key persons never knew about this return event. Oh, did I say that we were living in a professor's house. He never knew we had anything to do with any of this.

What can be the life application to the above incidents? First of all, I seemed to placing all the blame on the upperclassman assigned to me. Actually, I bought into the whole idea too. It sounded like fun to this teenager. When you are a part of something you shouldn't be a part of, don't shove the blame on others; accept your blame. Also, be man enough or woman enough to take a stand. If something is not right don't be a part of it, no matter the cost. Don't do as I did.

God tells us in Exodus 23:2, *"Do not follow the crowd in doing wrong…"* Deuteronomy 6:18 says, *"Do what is right and good in the Lord's sight…"* Simon Peter tells us in his first letter, 3:14, *"But even if you should suffer for what is right, you are blessed."* I'll mention one more biblical instruction that you and I should take to heart: *"Each one should test his own actions. Then he can take pride in himself, without comparing himself to everybody else, for each one should carry his own load"* (Galatians 6:4-5)

That thing you are considering with its questionable features – LEAVE IT ALONE!

The Thief Is Converted

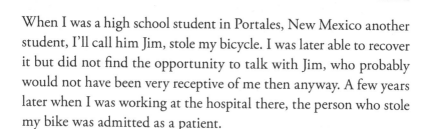

When I was a high school student in Portales, New Mexico another student, I'll call him Jim, stole my bicycle. I was later able to recover it but did not find the opportunity to talk with Jim, who probably would not have been very receptive of me then anyway. A few years later when I was working at the hospital there, the person who stole my bike was admitted as a patient.

God knows the future and His timing is right. I visited Jim in his room and was able to share God's good news with him. The following week a Baptist tent revival was to be conducted in Clovis, a city about 18 miles away. Jim agreed to go with me to the revival.

In the service Jim accepted Jesus Christ as his Savior. He went forward and made his decision public. The next step was to be baptized and join a church in Portales.

Before Jim was converted he had committed a felony and his trial was coming up. I talked to the judge, whom I knew personally, and informed him of Jim's conversion. At the trial, after the guilty sentence had been given the judge placed Jim on probation instead of sending him to jail. As far as I know, Jim remained true to his changed life in Christ.

When you are mistreated, Christ said to turn the other cheek. In other words, instead of fighting back or holding a grudge, show kindness. A grudge just changes you in a negative way. Kindness can change the other person, and you, in a positive way. It may be that God was just putting you in contact with someone who needed your kindness and to be shown God's love.

What about that neighbor? Uh oh, did I hit a soft spot?

It's not easy, but if you will show humility and seek to make things right, you can win a friend for life and he or she will be receptive of your words of God's love.

Jesus says in Matthew 5:38-39, *"You have heard it said, 'Eye for eye and tooth for tooth.' But I tell you, Do not resist an evil person. If someone strikes you on the right cheek, turn to him the other also."* If you react in kindness, the other person's anger is likely to melt. After all, even with our evil past and the way we have treated God, He still loves us so much that He sacrificed His Son to give us a new life here on earth and be with Him forever. Romans 5:8 says, *"But God demonstrates His love for us in this: While we were still sinners, Christ died for us."* No love is greater than that!

The Dog Swallowed His Bark

When I was a senior in high school in Cortez Colorado, I worked for a time in a hardware store. The whole front wall of the store was glass, including a glass door. One day the store owner's very small dog inside the store saw a large dog on the sidewalk out front. The small dog started following the outside one along the wall growling and barking as though he was ready to tear the large one to pieces. I thought, "My, what a brave little dog with a glass wall between them. I wonder what would happen if there was no wall." I went to glass door opened it. The little dog continued toward the door with its fierce bark. It arrived at the opening. Suddenly, with no wall separating them, they were face to face. The "brave" little fellow suddenly turned and started running away across the store yelping as though it was scared to death.

The dog was brave when it knew there was no danger. As soon as the situation changed its true nature was revealed. Do we sometimes put up a false front so others will see us in a better light than we deserve. I know there are some times that I have done that. In that way we can hide our true nature. I hope that is not true of you.

Some people who wear the name of Christian act one way when around other Christians, but at other times you would never know it. Their behavior and language is different. Where do you fit? The true believer's commitment is that Christ is his or her Lord. One's behavior is to be consistent and of a nature that will obey and honor Him.

OK, straighten up! Don't just depend on your own ability to do so. Repent and ask the Lord to help you. His Holy Spirit will guide you. He will warn you when you are tempted, convict you when you do wrong and encourage you when you remain true and obedient.

A prayer such as David prayed in the 25th Psalm is a good place to start. Verses 4 and 5 are as follows: *"Show me your ways, O Lord, teach me your paths; guide me in your truth and teach me, for you are God my Savior, and my hope is in you all day long."*

The message God gave to Jeremiah after he turned to the Lord for help will hold true for you. In Jeremiah 15:19 we find, *"Therefore this is what the Lord says, 'If you repent, I will restore you that you may serve me; ...'"* Jeremiah's service would be as God's spokesman to the Israelites. God has a plan for your life too.

There are three things you must do to know His plan for you. They are (1) Let God speak to you through His printed word, the Bible. This means you must read and study it. (2) Pray to God, asking Him for direction, and (3) listen to the Holy Spirit who will help you understand God's printed word and understand God's answers to your prayers. In all of this you must be receptive and obedient.

God may not reveal His full plan for you all at once. He may instill in you a caring concern for disadvantaged people and as that spirit matures show you a specific area of ministry relating to those with particular needs. If God calls you to a career ministry, you do not have to know all the specifics up front. You can start preparing yourself spiritually and professionally, perhaps in determining your college major, and then getting a seminary education. You can also start fulfilling whatever opportunities the Lord gives you now.

When I was in high school I thought God wanted me to be a missionary to Africa. He probably used an African missionary to instill in me the sense of a special calling and I jumped to that conclusion. However, I soon had opportunities for service. A church invited me to speak to their youth one Sunday night. As a senior I was asked to preach for some new congregations in a pioneer area.

Also, as a senior I was given the opportunity to preach a city-wide service in the football stadium.

God was using these occasions to impress on me that He was calling me to a pastoral ministry. I chose to go to a Baptist university in Oklahoma, then to a state university in New Mexico that had a Department Religion. These courses were offered through three Christian Chairs of Religion. Each chair, or center, owned its own property adjacent to the campus and paid its own professors. One of those centers was the Baptist Bible Chair. The courses were listed in the bulletin along with the rest. I was able to major in religion, taking Bible and biblical language courses. Also church pastorates were opened for me while I was a student. More intensive seminary study followed.

If you try to set your own course, you may build an empire consisting of things you like, and boast of your success. You will not be happy for long and could be like the dog that ran away howling. At least you may feel like it. If you are not doing what God wants of you, you will be aware that something is missing. In the early 1960's I made a departure from the preaching ministry for a time, into the pharmaceutical area. I was always aware that I was not where God wanted me. He finally got me to a place, the hospital ICU, where I would listen to Him.

So, let God show you what His plan for you is and pursue it! And stick with it.

My Video Doorbell

Several months ago I purchased and installed a video doorbell. It allows one-way video and two-way audio. I can also set it to record and notify me of any motion in quite a large area. I turned off that part because the street is near enough to my front door that I would be checking my smart phone too open. However, when the doorbell rings I am notified and can see the visitor drive into the driveway and walk to the door, then ring the bell.

If I am away, perhaps in another state, and the visitor is a stranger, I can simply say, "I cannot come to the door right now; how can I help you?" If I am interested I can give a time that would be more convenient. Otherwise, I could simply say, "I'm really not interested, but have a good day." The caller does not have to know that I'm not at home. If the caller is a friend and someone I trust, I can let the person know when I will be home. Also, even without a caller I can view a fairly large area in front of the house through the doorbell any time I want.

With this doorbell I must make a decision when it rings. I could make a bad decision by telling the wrong person that I'm not at home, and find things missing when I return. A good decision could be to listen to a friend who stopped to inform me that I had forgotten to turn off the sprinkler when I left town.

In life we are constantly faced with decisions. Sometimes they are either good or bad depending on our responses. To sell a product or service, you might tell the prospective customer all the advantages but neglect to mention some key disadvantage – a bad decision. The person in front of you at the fast food has trouble finding the money to pay for his/her order and you volunteer to supply the needed cash or pay for the full meal – a good decision.

Some decisions have moral implications and others have caring implications. The decisions you make will either please or displease the Lord. Sometimes God gives you the opportunity to share the good news of Christ. You must say, "Yes I will" or "No I won't." How often does this doorbell ring in your life?

When God confronted Cain who was angry because his offering was not accepted but his brother's was, He told Cain in Genesis 4:7, *"If you do what is right, will you not be accepted? But if you do not do what is right, sin is crouching at your door; it desires to have you, but you must master it."* Satan often rings our doorbells, but we must not let him in. God also rings. Let Him in. His news will be good for you. Isaiah 5:7 says, *"How beautiful on the mountains are the feet of those who bring good news, who proclaim peace, who bring good tidings, who proclaim salvation, who say to Zion, 'Your God reigns!'"*

Are your feet beautiful or ugly in God's sight? Wash them regularly by doing what is right!

One Pastor, Five Churches

One year I was invited to preach at a Baptist Church in Port Maria of Saint Mary, Jamaica. As I recall, the audience consisted of about 200 people, but only one car was in the parking lot. It belonged to a government worker. People either walked to church or caught one of the minibuses.

The pastor had five churches under his responsibility. Lay ministers would preach the four Sundays he could not be present. I was there on one of those Sundays. Nora, my wife, was the only White person in the congregation. When introducing her I said, "In case you do not know who my wife is, she is the one in the red dress." The people seemed to have a good sense of humor.

With the lack of street lights, Wednesday night Bible studies were conducted in homes. It seems that the membership residence areas were established for this. We were also able to attend one of these.

I wish all of our churches had the commitment and energy of that church in Jamaica! Everything they did was with enthusiasm – their singing, speaking and conversations. They seemed to enjoy worship and fellowship with one another.

How committed are you to your church. The people are the church and we are told in Hebrews 10:25, *"Let us not give up meeting together, as some are in the habit of doing, but let us encourage one another – and all the more as you see the Day approaching."*

Do you find excuses for skipping meeting with the rest of the church for worship, discipleship and fellowship? A former deacon of an area church once told me, "I don't attend anymore. I was a deacon for several years and I've served my time." It's easy to find excuses if you are looking for them. I guess the members of the church in Jamaica could easily say, "I don't want to walk two miles for a couple of hours at church." On the contrary, they seemed united and enthusiastic.

Speaking of united, do you tend to see faults here and there in the church, or do you see the positives and build on them? Paul, in writing to the Corinthian church said in 1 Corinthians 1:10, *"I appeal to you brothers, in the name of our Lord Jesus Christ, that all of you agree with one another so that there may be no divisions among you and that you may be perfectly united in mind and thought."* This does not mean everyone must have the same idea of the church's ministry events, etc., but be willing to give and take that for unity's sake. When the church makes a decision for a course of action, for instance, join in, be supportive and participate even though you would have gone another route. Help the church to be of one mind.

Got it? Halleluiah!

He Got a New Leg

While I was serving as director of missions for two associations in Maryland, we had a ministry in several migrant camps. The workers in these camps consisted mostly of men from Jamaica who had come to harvest the fruit in the orchards. One of the workers named Roy, a solid Christian, had a serious accident after returning to Jamaica one year. While riding his motorbike he was struck by a minibus and had to have his leg amputated from just below the knee.

Roy had lost his wife about two weeks before the accident and was left with six children. He would have to buy the uniforms and textbooks for each child to use at school, plus pay for their lunches. Unemployment was very high in Jamaica and it would be almost impossible for Roy to secure a job with his disability.

The time for all of this was only a few weeks before Christmas. I contacted some churches in the association in which the camp was located and they came up with a sum of money for getting Roy a new leg and for setting up a bank account in Jamaican to help him start his own business. Nora and I went to Jamaica and made all the arrangements for the leg and bank account. Also, Christmas presents for him and all of his children were sent along with us.

The pastor of the Baptist Church at Port Maria in Saint Mary went with us to take Roy across the island to the Medical Center in Kingston. There Roy was measured for an artificial leg. On the way back to Ocho Rios, where our hotel was located, we stopped and watched a championship soccer game.

Roy had been a member of a church in another denomination,

but after his injury the church seemed to lose interest in him. The Baptist church took him under their wing and Roy became a member there.

The trip was successful and satisfying. The Lord's hand was seen in everything that took place. Weverton Baptist Church in one of my associations took a special interest in Roy and invited him back to be with them for two weeks each year. I'm not sure how many years that lasted, as I now live in Texas.

In 1 John 3:17 we are told, *"If anyone has material possessions and sees his brother in need but has no pity on him, how can the love of God be in him?"* In the story of the Good Samaritan (Luke 10:30-35), Jesus shows us how we are to act toward those with special needs. This man stopped and helped a stranger of another culture who had been beaten and robbed, even though some "religious" guys had passed him by. Jesus Himself gave us the greatest example by His own actions. He regularly reached out to help those in need. Then He even went to the cross for you and me.

Let's follow His example. Open up your billfold and exert some energy! OK?

A Ball field for the Girls

When I was pastor of First Baptist Church in Kingsville Maryland the church was sitting on an eleven acre plot of land. We discussed possible uses of the property for reaching out to the community. One use could be a community garden that would be maintained and reaped primarily by people with special needs. A second use could be an ice skating rink for winter months. An area could be enclosed with a six inch curb and filled with water. The temperature would take care of the rest. I have seen times when, from mid-December to mid-January the temperature never rose above 32 degrees, sometimes reaching several degrees below zero.

The community had eight girls' softball teams and they were short on places to play. So, the first thing we acted on was to provide a playing field.

Since the field would be used by the community, the Army Corps of Engineers volunteered to develop it. They did a first class job, providing a nice backstop and benches. Pictures were taken and the  Baltimore Sun did a feature on it, showing the government, church and community working together.

At the end of the season to show their appreciation the girls provided eight trees positioned along each side of the lane leading from the street to the church. The community knew the church cared!

After eight years as pastor at Kingsville, I was called to be the director of missions for two associations in the state. I do not recall that either of the other potential plans for the community was ever attempted.

How is your church showing the community that it cares? Given its environment, what are the possibilities? Has the church ever stopped to explore the opportunities?

In Colossians 4:5 we are told, *"Be wise in the way you act toward outsiders; make the most of every opportunity."* Ephesians 4:12 states, *"... to prepare God's people for works of service, so that the body of Christ may be built up."* I believe a church's involvement in the community helps to strengthen the body of Christ, the church. Also I am convinced that some in the community become more receptive to the gospel of Christ.

So, ask God to show you the way and get started!

Presidential Visits

As I mentioned in another item, Camp David was in one of the associations I directed in Maryland. When we started a church in Thurmont, five miles from David the president's retreat, our Sunday school director, song leader and a teacher were all stationed at the camp. When Jimmy Carter was president, sometimes he would visit a church in the association. He would participate along with the rest of the congregation.

I was told that prior to the president's visit three churches would be contacted and inspected by an advance crew. They would even check entrances to the attic and put a security tape across the opening, so that if the tape were broken, the attic would have to be checked again. On Saturday evening the pastor of the church to be visited would be called. I never had the privilege of being where the president was attending as I was committed to preach in another church each time.

Whether a person agrees or disagrees with President Carter's political views, he was a man of character. There was no question about his Christian commitment. Even after his retirement from the presidency, he has been very active in humanitarian projects.

The president and others who lead our nation have an important impact on the country. It is important that we elect officials who hold to biblical principles and are willing to use their influence to right the wrongs that plague us.

The recorded history of Israel in the Bible reveals that when the nation was ruled by leaders who were faithful to the Lord, the country followed their example. The contrary happened when led by rulers who ignored Him. Of course the changes would not happen overnight, but the direction for change would be established.

On every level of government, local to national, let's learn the positions of the candidates for office as they relate to important biblical principles, such as abortion and same sex marriage and religious freedom. Then vote for those who hold to biblical principles. Psalm 33:12 tells us, *"Blessed is the nation whose God is the Lord..."* Proverbs 14:34 says, *"Righteousness exalts a nation, but sin is a disgrace to any people."*

If you love the Lord, show it by your vote!

The Jump Spark Works

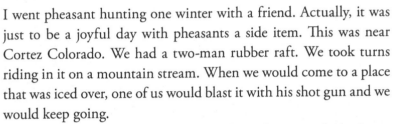

I went pheasant hunting one winter with a friend. Actually, it was just to be a joyful day with pheasants a side item. This was near Cortez Colorado. We had a two-man rubber raft. We took turns riding in it on a mountain stream. When we would come to a place that was iced over, one of us would blast it with his shot gun and we would keep going.

Once when it was my turn to be on the raft I sat on the back rim instead of on the bottom. The raft flipped over and I was drenched. We began hiking back to the car. Before reaching it my clothes were frozen and stiff. We had not brought any matches with us for building a fire.

I remembered that between my 9th and 10th years of high school I did dry land planting on a ranch in New Mexico. I would see smokers lighting their cigarettes by a jump spark on their tractors. A jump spark is made by removing the distributor wire from the plug and placing it a short distance from the plug's connector, then starting the engine. With the engine running, the person would hold his cigarette between the plug and the wire's connector to light it.

So, we gathered up sticks and got ready for a fire. I removed the oil filter from the carburetor on the 1937 Pontiac and inserted a tiny corner of a piece of paper into the carburetor to get some gasoline on it. I then made a jump spark and inserted that corner of the paper between the plug and the connector on the wire. It caught fire and we lit the sticks. We quickly had a nice fire and I thawed and dried out.

A few years later, after I was married and before we had children, Nora and I went to Carlsbad, New Mexico to go through the caverns. We took sleeping bags and slept in the park. The next morning we planned to fix our breakfast on one of the grills in the park, but I had failed to bring matches. The jump spark trick worked again!

Sometimes we are faced with situations which seem impossible to solve. Don't give up. Have you heard the expression, "Where there's a will, there's a way"? For the Christian, the way is the Lord. We can always go to Him. He will know all about the problem. He will listen to you and show you the right way to address the situation.

Moses could have given up when he was leading the Israelites out of Egypt and came to the sea, with the Egyptian army behind him. But he had faith that God would see them through and God opened up the water and let them cross over.

Two blind men once asked Jesus to help them. According to Matthew 9:28-30 *"He asked them, 'Do you believe that I am able to do this?' 'Yes, Lord,' they replied. Then He touched their eyes and said, 'According to your faith will it be done to you.'; and their sight was restored."*

Just trust the Lord to guide you through life's situations. The answer and solution may not always be what you would prefer, but God knows the future and will lead you in the way that is best.

Different Language but Shared Faith

When I was an associational director of missions in Maryland, I had the privilege of helping Christians from other countries and languages establish local congregations here in the United States. Many different language groups are located in Maryland and the D.C. area. In fact, the largest Southern Baptist Church in the Maryland/Delaware convention is a Korean congregation located in a Maryland suburb of Washington D.C. I remember one year when the state's annual convention was held there.

In one of the associations which I directed we eventually had Korean, Vietnamese and Chin tribe congregations. I was able to help the Koreans find locations for their congregations to meet, worked with our embassy in Korea and U.S. representative in helping to bring a pastor to one of the congregations.

A Vietnamese congregation was established as a mission of one of our churches. I also had the privilege of helping Christians from the Chen tribe in Myanmar (Burma) understand how to form a congregation and secure a place for meeting.

It was a pleasure working with each of these. Each group had at least one person who understood and spoke English fairly well. When I had the privilege of preaching to one of these congregations, they would have a bi-lingual person interpret. When simply attending the service, they would have the bi-lingual person sit with Nora and me to keep us up on what the pastor was saying.

In at least one of our associational gatherings, we handed out headphones to the non-English speaking attendees. These had the ability to select the language. Interpreters were in the back of the auditorium to provide the input.

These congregations would generally have a meal following their Sunday morning service. The Koreans bow in greeting one another. They bow more deeply to ministers. I always returned the bow. When eating with them after a service, they would hold their children back until visitors had gone through the line. On our first visit or two, they had someone to go along with Nora and me and explain each food item. The Koreans were very respectful people. When visiting in their homes Nora and I would always remove our shoes, as was their practice.

These churches were also connected to a Korean Baptist Association. Sometimes that association would have a ministers' conference in our area and invite me. There was always a meal. I would use chopsticks. That's all they used. For awhile they would bring eating utensils to me. Soon they stopped doing that, as I got comfortable with chopsticks.

The Korean churches, in the associations where I served, gathered at 5:30 in the morning for prayer before going to work. But they do this in their own country as well. In one of my missions classes at the seminary, one of the students told of an experience he had. It was during the Korean Conflict. He was on patrol duty and it was not quiet daylight. He heard a noise of many voices just over the hill. He went to investigate. There he found several hundred Christians who had gathered for prayer before starting the general activities of the day. No wonder the Christian populace among the Koreans continues to grow dramatically. We had a great time and it was a pleasure working with these language groups.

The Lord provides us with various kinds of ministries. These may include, language groups (including the deaf), resort ministries, the handicapped, or the next door neighbor or a coffee group. He has provided an opportunity for you. If you are disabled, it may be a prayer ministry He has for you, or the use of the telephone or email. Every Christian is called to be a witness. He may call you to share with someone who has a physical need, providing the opportunity to share the gospel. God has a plan for your life. Share the good news of Jesus Christ!

Hebrews 13:15-16 tells us, *"Through Jesus, therefore, let us continually offer to God a sacrifice of praise – the fruit of lips that confess His name. And do not forget to do good and to share with others, for with such sacrifices God is pleased."*

Jesus gave us what is known as the Great Commission in Matthew 28:19-20. There He said, *"...All authority in heaven and on earth has been given to me. Therefore go and make disciples of all nations, baptizing them in the name of the father and of the Son and of the Holy Spirit, and teaching them to obey everything I have commanded you. And surely I am with you always, to the very end of the age."*

What specifically is God's plan for you? Are you obeying Him? Then get busy. Ask God for the next assignment. He will guide you through it!

All Greek to Me

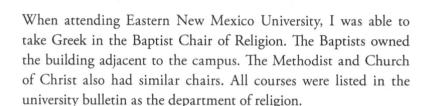

When attending Eastern New Mexico University, I was able to take Greek in the Baptist Chair of Religion. The Baptists owned the building adjacent to the campus. The Methodist and Church of Christ also had similar chairs. All courses were listed in the university bulletin as the department of religion.

I enjoyed the course and after the first semester a friend who also was in the class and I walked the same direction to lunch. We agreed between us that on the way to lunch we would speak to one another only in Greek – a switch in the expression, "It's all Greek to me." Wow! The conversations were not very fluid. Because of our walking conversations, our after class studies were increased. Where there were problems, we found the answers. Assignments and tests became easier.

Understanding the Greek language opens up the Scripture in a way that English sometimes fails. For instance, and I may have mentioned this in another item in this book, when Jesus was on the cross, He said, *"Father, forgive them for they do not know what they are doing"* (Luke 23:34). The Greek tense of the word for "said" here is an iterative imperfect. That means this was the final of a series of times He had asked for their forgiveness. Perhaps when He was taken by those who acted on Judas' betrayal, he said "Father forgive them; they don't know what this is all about." He may have said something similar at each phase of his trial.

Another important clarification from the Greek manuscript is in John 3:16, familiar to most of us. Because of its importance I will repeat here an explanation I have included elsewhere. In the phrase *"... whoever believes in Him shall not parish but have eternal life"* the word *"in"* could have used either of two Greek words. One is, using English characters, *"en"* which is illustrated by a circle and an arrow going around it. That means to believe about something. The word that was used is *"eis."* That is illustrated by a circle with an arrow going through it. If it made good English, the wording could be "whoever believes into Him." That would mean whoever trusts Him.

I could look at a chair and note that it was well constructed and say, "I believe it would hold my weight." That is just believing in, or something about, the chair. I could sit in it, trusting it with my weight. That would capture the meaning of the word used in the Greek manuscript in John 3:16.

What if you have no opportunity to learn Greek? Though a paraphrase should not be one's primary study Bible because often the author's opinion is included, which may or may not be true to the original manuscript, a good paraphrase can be a helpful tool in getting more to the original meaning of some of the passages. Also a good Bible commentary, available at a Christian book store, can be a great help. Do not let these instances discourage you from studying one of the basic translations. You can trust what you read. The occasional variances simply expand some of the meanings.

Planting Seeds

One time when I was flying from Alabama to Dallas, I sat next to a Hindu man from India. He lived in Dallas. We talked about his work in the computer industry. Then I asked him about the Hindu religion and let him share with me about his faith. After that I was able to share with him about the Christian faith and eternal life, not just a reappearing of life in another form. He indicated that he had attended a Baptist church in Dallas a few times. But he was not ready for a decision to change.

I planted some seeds, or perhaps watered or cultivated what others had planted. Later, someone may reap the harvest.

When you share the good news of Christ with someone and do not receive the results you had hoped for, do not be discouraged. You were a faithful witness. You are responsible for sharing; the other person is responsible for the response. You may have started the person thinking about his or her direction in life. The seed is planted. It may take someone to water and someone to reap.

The apostle Paul told the Corinthians, *"I planted the seed, Apollos watered it, but God made it grow"* (1 Corinthians 3:6).

Being Salt

Jesus tells us that His followers are the salt of the earth. Salt is a preservative. It is used to prevent decay. We as Christians are the salt that will prevent or arrest moral and spiritual decay in this world. We are to use the opportunities God gives us, in the context of our experiences.

One of the best examples I know, was a pastor who served a church in one of my associations in Maryland. He was only about 40 years old but he contracted leukemia. After receiving the bone marrow transplant, he got an infection and died before leaving the hospital. Through the year before the transplant he looked healthy but he knew the clock was ticking on his life. I kept in close contact with Bert and his family.

During the drives for donors, the television stations in the Baltimore area covered him closely with at least weekly updates. We saw him at the hospital in Kentucky, and there both the Lexington and Baltimore stations covered the story. Even as we went to the cemetery, all along the way news cameras were stationed by the road. In that year before his death, the television reporters would ask him questions such as this: "Aren't you mad at God for letting you have this dread disease at such an early age?" Bert would reply something like this, "Why should I be mad at God. He has been good to me. He has given me a loving, faithful wife, a beautiful family and a caring congregation to pastor. What more could I want?" His witness was always positive without being preachy. He made following Christ attractive. He was the kind of salt Jesus was talking about.

Not only is salt a preservative, it is a seasoning, making the unpalatable tasty. And salt is essential to life. A low sodium content can cause all kinds of problems in the body. God's plan for redemption of the world includes you and me. Let us be pure and useful salt. Here are Jesus' words in Matt. 5:13, *"You are the salt of the earth. But if the salt loses its saltiness, how can it be made salty again? It is no longer good for anything, except to be thrown out and trampled by men."*

Jesus was telling his disciples that they were the preservative and the seasoning in the degenerating and unpalatable world. He is telling us today, "Season the world with all of your seasoning qualities." We must be aware of our influence upon those about us and conduct our own lives in a responsible way before God.

Calling a Pastor?

When I was a director of missions a pastor was called to one of my churches that seemed to be thriving and have every opportunity for a fruitful ministry, but he was not given the whole story. The church had just split down the middle over its termination of the previous pastor. Financial obligations had been made that it now could not meet.

The new pastor and his family came from another state into a hotbed they were not prepared for. The pastor told me, "I do not have the background or training or experience to deal adequately with these issues. If the church had been honest with me, I would either have not come or suggested that they first spend some time with a good interim pastor to deal with these issues, so that when a pastor is called, he can start off on a positive note & lead the church in a productive way."

The new pastor, who did not see himself as called to be an interim pastor, essentially had to serve in that role, deal with the issues the best he could, and then see the church call another pastor to start fresh.

If your church is in the process of making a leadership change, it's a good time to take an inward look. Hang on to the positives and improve them. Also decide how you will deal with the negatives. Be honest. Be open. Be patient with one another. Be good listeners. Be forgiving. Be flexible. Be honest with a prospective pastor. Be open to the leadership of the Lord Jesus Christ.

Paul, in providing help to the church in Rome, told them, *"May the God who gives endurance and encouragement give you a spirit of unity among yourselves as you follow Christ Jesus, so that with one heart and mouth you may glorify the God and Father of our Lord Jesus Christ"* (Romans 15:5-6).

Blind but a
Powerful Ministry

One November Nora & I made a trip from Texas to Maryland. I had been invited to share at the annual association meeting. I had been director of the association for twenty years until my retirement.

We returned home through KY where there was a camp for blind children. Mike Gates, a blind man, was the director and his wife, Lori, assisted him.

Mike was probably in his early forties when we visited. When he was 12 years old he and a friend were hunting and the friend's gun went off and took out both of Mike's eyes. But Mike later saw this as God giving him a special ministry.

My wife Nora belonged to an international quilting group which had made fifty quilts for the fifty beds in the camp. Each quilt had a design and a scripture verse that could be read by the touch. We arrived on the first day of the deer season and Mike was going deer hunting. That's right! How?

The camp was deep in the forest and Mike had built a deer stand, about three by six feet, if I remember correctly, on the side of a tree. It was about six or eight feet from the ground. First, when hunting with a gun, he needs another person holding a laptop computer. The sight on the gun sends the sighted target to the laptop. When the sight is in the right spot, he has his deer.

Second, when using the bow and arrow, Mike doesn't need another person's help. Near the deer stand he had constructed a low J-shaped rock fence. He would put carrots in the curved end of the J, as deer are the only large animal of the forest that will eat carrots. To learn the right spot to shoot, he first had a small circle placed where the vital spot on the deer would be located. He said he practiced until he could shoot fifty times through the circle. Mike told me that a deer will come along and look over the fence, but is too lazy to reach over it for the food. The deer will then come around into the J and he said, "When I hear the crunching of the carrots, they are mine."

In each two week camp for blind children, Mike teaches archery to them and they have a petting zoo on location. But the main purpose of the camp is the Bible teaching and Christian instruction he and Lori do. Many children accept Jesus as their Savior.

Often you may face challenges and difficulties in life. You might ask if God is guiding you into something special He has for you. Seek His direction. Concern for others led Mike and Lori to commit their lives to Christ's Outreach for the Blind. Scores of volunteers also help in this ministry. What does God have waiting for you?

What Paul tells the Roman church also applies to us: *"Be devoted to one another in brotherly love. Honor one another above yourselves. Never be lacking in zeal, but keep your spiritual fervor, serving the Lord. Be joyful in hope, patient in affliction, faithful in prayer"* (Romans 12: 10-12a).

In 2 Timothy 2:15 Paul tells us, *"Do your best to present yourself to God as one approved, a workman who does not need to be ashamed and who correctly handles the word of truth."*

Does What Others Think Matter?

For a time in the 1950's I was an insurance salesman. It was for a debit insurance company. The policy holders had premiums that they could pay weekly, monthly, annually, or for any number of weeks they wished. These were personally picked up by the salesperson. Most collections were at homes. However, some of the policyholders worked in bars or pool halls and it was necessary for me to enter those places to collect the premiums.

As people would see me enter those businesses, and someone I knew might be there, I was concerned about my testimony and sometimes wondered what I should do about my work. Other Christians are engaged in work that takes them into places that could cause people to wonder about their faith & commitment. There are life situations, other than work, that may cause the same concerns.

Some Christians are constantly aware of what others think and this determines many of their actions. Others seem never to consider what other people think, but still go about their way trying to live responsibly before God. They seem to give no thought to what others may think about where they go or what they do.

The big question is this: How much attention should Christians give to what others think? This is a decision you must make. I will provide some things to consider, but the decision must be yours.

Here is some of the Apostle Paul's advice: In 1 Timothy 4:12 he says, *"Don't let anyone look down on you because you are young, but set an example for the believers in speech, in life, in love, in faith and in purity."* Then in 1 Thessalonians 4:11-12 he says, *"Make it your ambition to lead a quiet life, to mind your own business and to work with your hands, just as we told you, so that your daily life may win the respect of outsiders and so that you will not be dependent on anybody."*

The question I have imposed will include every area of life – What others think about what you say or do, where you go, what you wear, who you associate with, and whatever else you may think of. Should any consideration be given to what others think?

How do you reconcile Jesus' actions? He was often found at the banquet table of Pharisees and was the friend of immoral women. Some received the impression that He was a wine bibber. For instance, at the wedding in Cana Jesus made more wine when the host ran out. If it was non-toxic, the others didn't know.

Yet Paul was considerate of others when he talked about eating meat offered to idols. Colossians 4:5 tells us to *"Be wise in the way you act toward outsiders. Make the most of every opportunity."*

When I had to enter places I did not wish to go, to collect insurance premiums, I had witnessing opportunities I would not have elsewhere, although I'm sure I passed up many more opportunities than I took advantage of.

So, let's take another look at our question, with a slightly different perspective. To what extent should others control your life? You can come to the place that you are merely living the lives of others, and not your own life. So, the question for which you must decide the answer: Where is the proper balance to be drawn?

Ephesians 5:15 says, *"Be very careful then, how you live – not as unwise but as wise."*

She Was Angry With God

When I was a pastor in Dallas, I remember a lady who was angry with God because He allowed her Christian mother to suffer over a period of time with cancer before taking her home. God can handle the anger, and He is willing to help one through it. But this lady turned from God and His church. It may be that God wanted to help her develop a caring spirit and patience, and finally a joy that He took her to a place where she would no longer suffer. If she had looked to the Lord, He would have seen her through the difficult time and strengthened her faith. But her intense, unrelenting anger blocked access to those benefits.

When life deals severe blows where do you turn? – To self in pity? To taking shortcuts? To making unethical decisions? Or to the Lord?

From a human point of view, it seems that some persons & families receive more than their share of tragedy and suffering. Some become bitter and blame God. They turn from Him and His church. Others are melted and turn to God as never before.

Our Lord cares for us. When we hurt, He hurts. He wills what is best for us. He does not isolate us from the hurts common to man, but He does promise us Himself in the midst of those trials. We do not have to face them alone. He will bring healing, supply strength and walk through the valley with us. 1 Peter 5:7 tells us, *"Cast all your anxiety on Him because He cares for you."*

He Gave a Kidney

When I was a director of missions in Maryland, the pastor of a church in one of my associations reflected the example of Jesus who gave Himself for us. His father-in-law who was not a Christian needed a kidney. This pastor, Howard, offered one of his kidneys. He hoped this giving up a part of himself would help his father-in-law to be more receptive to the gospel and salvation. The Lord honored this sacrifice and a few months later, his father-in-law accepted Jesus Christ as his Savior.

In John 15:12-13 Jesus said, *"My command is this: Love each other as I have loved you. Greater love has no one than this, that he lay down his life for his friends."* Howard did not lay down his life but he did sacrifice a part of his body. Who knows, someday he may need that other kidney. What a witness!

Christ did lay down His life for us. After Jesus had acted as a servant and washed his disciples' feet, he said, *"I have set you an example that you should do as I have done for you. I tell you the truth, no servant is greater than his master, nor is a messenger greater than the one who sent him. Now that you know these things, you will be blessed if you do them"* (John 13:15-17).

Sometimes it isn't easy for us to follow Christ's example, but many have even given their lives for the sake of the gospel of Christ. How far would you go?

A Church is Started

When Nora and I arrived in Maryland in 1969, Southern Baptists made up about 2.5% of the population. Many areas of the state were without an evangelical church. After I became the director of missions in 1975, we established a Bible study fellowship in the growing city of Taneytown and secured Westminster Baptist Church as the church sponsor. That small group soon found a vacated store building right on the town square intersection of the 2 highways through town.

I served as interim pastor until a pastor was secured. Home Mission funds paid part of the pastor's salary on a phase out basis, reducing 20% each year as the congregation grew and constituted into a church. With rent assistance from the state convention and Home Mission Board, the storefront served until it became necessary to purchase property and build. A Home Missions loan made that possible. The Southern Baptist organization then called the Home Mission Board was later re-named the North American Mission Board. Today that church in Taneytown is a strong congregation in Carroll County, MD.

God calls people as missionaries here in our United States, as He does in the other parts of the world. Some areas of our nation have very little evangelical witness. If God should ask you to move to a state where there is a great need, leaving your family and friends, would you be willing to go? He calls some people to move to a foreign country, often without the opportunity of seeing their loved ones at home until their furlough in the seventh year of service. Remember the hymn, "Wherever He Leads, I'll Go"? Would you?

Jesus told us in Matthew 28:19-20, *"Therefore go and make disciples of all nations, baptizing them in the name of the Father and of the Son and of the Holy Spirit, and teaching them to obey everything I have commanded you. And surely I am with you always, to the very end of the age."*

Church Start Near Camp David

The second congregation we started after becoming director of missions of two associations in Maryland was in Thurmont, just 5 miles from Camp David, the president's retreat. We secured a missions group of students and adults from Georgia and arranged four Backyard Bible clubs in different areas of the city where there were children. A pavilion in the city park was reserved and a music concert was conducted for the city by the mission group on Saturday night.

The Bible clubs were followed up by visitation and newspaper ads for a service in the band room at the high school. After moving from place to place, we found a building in an excellent location from which an appliance store had just moved. I served as interim pastor until Myersville Baptist, the sponsoring church, provided a pastor. Mission funds helped in all of this.

Property next to the elementary school was secured and a first unit built. As I mentioned in another item, the pianist, Sunday school director, song leader and a teacher were all from Camp David. Five churches agreed to assist, and the sponsoring church set up a schedule for families who would volunteer to attend for a month. To the best of my recollection, about 4 families would visit for a month and place their tithes there. This would be repeated each month for a while. If a Sunday school teacher was needed, a volunteer would commit 3 months. Several churches provided special music.

Some Baptists who had moved to the area from southern states began to attend. The church related to the community in a positive way and it continued to grow. Soon the outside volunteers were no longer needed. Baptisms were conducted in a nearby stream until a permanent building with a baptistery was built. Many people became believers and were discipled.

After about a year, the association developed a booklet produced by the new congregation. It contained census data for Thurmont, services for new comers to the city such as doctors and dental offices, laundry, all the churches and other information. The City Hall was kept supplied with them and they were distributed to new move-ins as they sought information or conducted business at the city offices. This helped people know that First Baptist Church was an active part of the community.

We are all called to serve and the Lord may have a place for you in taking the gospel to people in areas where there is a lack of an evangelical witness. Have you considered this?

Jesus said in John 12:26, *"Whoever serves me must follow me; and where I am my servant will be. My Father will honor the one who serves me."*

The Manger was in a Cave

Some years ago, Nora and I were in Bethlehem. We saw a manger that could be the one in which the baby Jesus was placed; if not, it must have been similar to it. Unlike the popular conception of Jesus' manger, the stable we were in was in a cave and the manger, or feed trough, was hewn out of stone. A large water container for the livestock, also hewn out of a large stone, was at the end of the manger. There was plenty of room for the shepherds' visit. Caves were often used as stables. The site of the one I referred to is in an appropriate location to be the one in which Jesus was born.

The area was covered with caves, many very large. You perhaps recall that when Saul was pursuing David, he went into a cave and took a nap. This was a different cave, on the other side of the Jordan. Scripture tells us that David and his 600 men were far back in that cave. While Saul slept, David cut off a piece of his garment. When Saul was back with his army, David came out, held up the piece he had cut off and called out to Saul, "Is this yours, Saul?"

Visiting the manger and other biblical sights helped to bring the scriptural events more vividly to life. We had many awesome experiences. Out of our excitement, we can share with you and be convincing because we experienced it. We can cause you to want to go. But you will never fully grasp what we say until you experience it. It is the same with salvation. You & I can cause others to want it. When they experience it, they will understand. If you get a chance to visit the holy lands, be sure to go. You will not regret it.

A Lesson from the Birds

When Nora & I lived in Maryland, we would put seed out for the birds, especially in the winter when the ground was covered with snow. I would shovel out an area down to the grass, so the birds could pick up the seeds.

One Sunday morning as we were getting ready for church, Nora was looking out the bedroom window to the back yard. She said, Don, come here. I went to the window and could hardly believe my eyes. A group of 8 or 10 sparrows were feeding. One of them, a full-grown adult bird, had a malformed bill. It could not pick up the seeds. It would also be the last bird to lift off the ground when they would fly. It seemed that it might have been a mentally impaired bird. We saw at least 4 other birds pick up seeds and drop them into the open mouth of the impaired bird. I thought that among wildlife, the law was just the survival of the fittest. I had never seen this type of caring among birds.

As I pondered about what we had just witnessed, I thought, "This is the way the church fellowship should be." It should be a closely-knit caring family. When one hurts, the entire fellowship hurts & reaches out to that one. When someone receives a special blessing, rejoice.

Paul said to the church at Thessalonica, *"We ought always to thank God for you, because your faith is growing more and more, and the love every one of you has for each other is increasing"* (2 Thessalonians 1:3). The church is to be a fellowship of love; guard it. You are family. There will be differences among you from time to time, as there is in any family. Settle the differences promptly and forgive one another. Do not try to fit one another into your own straight jacket, but let each one be responsible before God.

God made each of you a unique person. Each of you is different from anyone else. You have different backgrounds, different skills, different experiences, different ideas and different emotional and mental make-ups. All of this will affect how you look at things. It also means that you each have something to contribute. You can learn from one another and make better group decisions. It's OK not to agree on everything. Allow it. Always address issues & ideas, not persons.

Caring people can disagree without damaging their relationships. Isn't it a relief when we free ourselves from trying to be judges of one another? Judging is God's business. Our business is to share His love & point people to Him & get our lives in line with His will.

Where is Your Focus?

I remember when we lived in Fort Worth my witnessing partner, a devoted businessman, and I were talking to a young man who claimed to be a Christian. He was the leader of a band playing for night clubs. This was only one of his jobs. He was a talented man with an outstanding singing voice. He had just produced a record. We talked to him about letting his life count for Christ and using his talents for Christ. This young man said, "I want to, but first I want to be able to provide some nice things for my family and the money is in the night clubs." Possession of things had become an end in itself.

What do you want out of life? What goals are you striving for? What is the motivating factor behind your ambitions? Is it money? Is it promotion in your work? Is it gaining more of the worlds goods? Is it to gain a position of prestige? Or is it to honor Christ wherever he puts you?

Materialism as an end in itself and Christianity are roads going in opposite directions. Your primary objective and focus in life should not be the accumulation of wealth and status. Of course the Christian must be dependable and faithfully shoulder his or her responsibilities. Then increased income and promotion may come to you and you can see them as God's blessings. This principle applies whether you are employed by someone else, self-employed, retired or a stay-at-home mom.

Young people, you need to commit to this principle now and as you start your work careers & life commitments. For many young people popularity and acceptance are all important. Just be true to the Lord Jesus Christ and these things will take care of themselves. They must not be your top priority. Your top priority is to be true to Christ and his calling for your life.

Jesus said, *"But seek first His kingdom and His righteousness, and all these things will be given to you as well"* (Matthew 6:29).

Cliff Dwellings Were Their Homes

A couple of months after Nora, my wife died in August, 2017, I took a ten day trip to New Mexico and Colorado exploring areas in which we had some great memories. This included a day among the cliff dwellings in Mesa Verde National Park, only about 7½ miles from Cortez, in southwest Colorado near the four corners area, the only place where four states come together.

Early Inhabitants, prior to the present day Ute tribes, were able to carve out multi-room living and meeting quarters in the cliff sides. The largest of these is named Cliff palace. It contains halls, rooms, and towers and it is estimated that it could house 100 people. According to the parks official website, mesaverde.com, the dwellings are the work of "the Ancestral Pueblo people who made it their home for over 700 years, from A.D. 600 to A.D. 1300. Today, Mesa Verde National Park protects over 4,000 known archeological sites, including 600 cliff dwellings."

It's amazing that the cliff dwellers could either climb up to, or down to the sites, much less have tools and space to carve out the magnificent living and meeting quarters. Of course, once at home they were probably safe from enemy intruders, including wild animals.

This was one of the highlights of my trip. There is a saying, "Where there is a will there is a way." The cliff dwellers had a will and found a way. One reason our nation and world are in the shape we are is the lack of will among Christians. We are the church, and the Lord has given us an assignment. Too few of us have taken the assignment seriously.

Do you know the spiritual situation of you neighbor? What about your family and extended family? Have all of them trusted the Lord and are they living a life that gives evidence to that? Have you witnessed to them? See what I mean. We know what we are instructed to do by our Lord but let so many obvious opportunities pass us by.

Jesus said, as recorded in Acts 1:8, *"But you will receive power when the Holy Spirit comes upon you; and you will be my witnesses in Jerusalem and in all Judea and Samaria, and to the ends of the earth."*

Conclusion

The Lord has been good to me throughout my whole 88 years. He placed me in a God-loving family, gave me a wonderful Christian wife and provided us with caring children who love the Lord and married Bible-believing spouses. Our grand children have been, and are a great blessing as well, and our great grandchildren are a real joy. All of my siblings have been active believers with Christian spouses and children.

I may have one day or a dozen more years on earth before the Lord calls me home. I simply wanted to publish this work to leave a continuing witness after I'm gone. I do not dread the day I go. It will be a glorious time. I will be able to see the Father and His Son Jesus, the prophets of old, the apostles and family members who have preceded me! And I'll see my wife again! God has something good in store for His children!

So, I hope you have enjoyed this little book and have received help in some areas of your life. So Audios, I'll look forward to seeing you in heaven.

About the Author

Having been born in 1930, Donald Brown lived through much of the Great Depression. His work history included life on the farm, a ranch hand, national sales director and vice president of a pharmaceutical company, pastor and director of missions.

In addition to the above work experiences, Don has lived in five states including time on an Indian reservation, in large cities and on a rural farm. He has traveled in the Near East, Europe and elsewhere. The varied experiences throughout his 88 years, dating from childhood, have brought about many interesting occurrences.

As to his education, Don received his BA degree at Eastern New Mexico University, the MDiv at Southwestern Baptist Theological Seminary and DMin from Midwestern Baptist Theological Seminary.

Each experience recorded in this work is followed by a life application and appropriate scripture. The author's purpose is to lead the reader to see God's protective and guiding hand in all of life's experiences.

Printed in the United States
By Bookmasters